Women Writers in Black Africa

Recent titles in
Contributions in Women's Studies

Women In Irish Society: The Historical Dimension
Margaret MacCurtain and Donncha O'Corrain

Margaret Fuller's *Woman in the Nineteenth Century:*
A Literary Study of Form and Content, of Sources and Influence
Marie Mitchell Olesen Urbanski

To Work and to Wed: Female Employment, Feminism, and the Great
Depression
Lois Scharf

Eve's Orphans: Mothers and Daughters in Medieval Literature
Nikki Stiller

Women, War, and Work: The Impact of World War I on Women Workers
in the United States
Maurine Weiner Greenwald

Self, Society, and Womankind: The Dialectic of Liberation
Kathy E. Ferguson

Women as Interpreters of the Visual Arts, 1820-1979
Claire Richter Sherman, editor, with Adele M. Holcomb

Flawed Liberation: Socialism and Feminism
Sally M. Miller, editor

Wartime Women: Sex Roles, Family Relations, and the Status of Women
During World War II
Karen Anderson

Women Writers in Black Africa

LLOYD W. BROWN

Contributions in Women's Studies, Number 21

GREENWOOD PRESS

WESTPORT, CONNECTICUT • LONDON, ENGLAND

Library of Congress Cataloging in Publication Data

Brown, Lloyd Weslesley, 1938-
    Women writers in Black Africa.

    (Contributions in women's studies ; no. 21 ISSN
0147-104X)
    Bibliography: p.
    1. African literature (English)—Women authors—
History and criticism. I. Title. II. Series.
PR9340.B7   820   80-1710
ISBN 0-313-22540-0 (lib. bdg.)

Library of Congress Catalog Card Number: 80-1710
ISBN: 0-313-22540-0
ISSN: 0147-104X

First published in 1981

Greenwood Press
A division of Congressional Information Service, Inc.
88 Post Road West
Westport, Connecticut 06881

Printed in the United States of America

10 9 8 7 6 5 4 3 2 1

Contents

Acknowledgments

Sections of this study appeared previously in *Umoja* (University of Colorado, Boulder), *World Literature Written in English* (University of Guelph, Ontario, Canada), and *Canadian Journal of African Studies* (Concordia University, Montreal). I wish to acknowledge the kind permission of the editors to use these materials. I also wish to acknowledge the kind permission of Heinemann Educational Books (London) to quote from the following: Flora Nwapa, *Efuru*, and Flora Nwapa, *Idu*.

Women Writers in
Black Africa

1 Introduction

The last twenty years has witnessed an explosive growth of interest in African literature. There has been an outpouring of anthologies, papers, and book-length studies. Heinemann's African Writers Series, out of the London publishing house, has been so thorough in bringing out works by new and established writers that it remains, without question, the most impressive undertaking of its kind in the publishing of Third World literature. Indeed, the study of African literature has become both a distinctly Third World undertaking— that is, the study of the literature in relation to Africa itself—and a comparative discipline, with increasing emphasis on the relationship between African literature, and Western and black literature in the Americas.

This kind of interest in African literature continues to grow, and there is every reason to believe that the voice of the African writer will be heard and studied for a long time to come, as artist, social analyst, and literary critic. But in all of this, African literature has to be understood as literature by African men, for interest in African literature has, with very rare exceptions, excluded women writers. The women writers of Africa are the other voices, the unheard voices, rarely discussed and seldom accorded space in the repetitive anthologies and predictably male-oriented studies in the field. Relatively few magazines and scholarly journals, in the West and in Africa itself, have found significant space or time for African women writers. The ignoring of women writers on the continent has become a tradition, implicit rather than formally stated, but a tradition nonetheless—and a rather unfortunate one at that.

The number of women writing in Africa has always been rather small when compared with their male counterparts. This imbalance reflects a truism in modern African history—that until relatively recently, women did not enjoy comparable educational opportunities, so that correspondingly fewer acquired the literacy, let alone the university education, that have traditionally been prerequisites for the writing of African literature in European languages. In this regard, women in the former British colonies seem to have fared better than those in other parts of colonial Africa, with the result that all women writers of any significance write in English. Small as the number of writers has been, it includes writers whose achievements are, at the very least, comparable with those male writers who are the invariable subjects of the customary discussions of literature.

It is an unquestionable fact, for example, that as teacher, producer, and writer Efua Sutherland has been a formidable and unequalled influence in the development of modern theater in Ghana. Flora Nwapa's two novels (*Efuru* and *Idu*) are two of the most imaginative and ambitious attempts, in Nigeria and Africa as a whole, to integrate oral forms with the literate design of the novel. At a time when protest themes on a variety of subjects still attract attention in African literature, irrespective of the literary merits involved, there has been a curious indifference to *female* voices of protest, like South Africa's Bessie Head or Nigeria's relative newcomer, Buchi Emecheta. Few writers anywhere on the continent have mastered the art of the short story as well as Ghana's Ama Ata Aidoo, but she has managed to attract only limited attention.

The rather cavalier dismissal of the woman writer in Africa is not altogether inexplicable. Indeed, some of its roots are familiar enough. African literature is often approached and heralded as one area that demands innovative criticism, free of some of the limitations of Western scholarship—"Eurocentrism" (or racism, to be blunt), an overly narrow preoccupation with nique to the exclusion of cultural themes and cultural co nsion. Notwithstanding this kind of fanfare, African litera criticism has always suffered from that male-oriented selectivity, or exclusivism, which it has inherited from the West and which has only recently been seriously challenged in the West itself. This does not mean that Western (male) scholars are solely to blame for the male orientation of much of

African studies (including literary criticism)—even though Western male Africanists have contributed heavily to an old boy network of African studies in which the African woman simply does not exist as a serious or significant writer. Africans and other black Africanists have just as selective in their basic assumptions about what constitutes African literature. As anthologists and critics they have treated their subject as if it were an exclusively male product, or preserve.

Neither has the neglect been entirely male. A recent study of the heroine in African literature, written by a woman, managed to discuss its subject without once giving the slightest inkling that women have contributed to the literature, and to the literature's diverse ideas of female heroism. In this case, the lack of any reference to the woman writer in Africa seems to be based on a disturbing and profound ignorance. We are asked to believe that "the near invisibility of the African woman as heroine" in the literature has been caused by colonialism (which "diminished" the "inalienable rights and prerogatives" of women), rather than by the "mores of traditional African society."[1] What is disturbing is the patently false assumption that images of women in African literature are all limited, and that this limitation is due solely to colonialism. It does not take a great deal of diligence, or knowledge about the subject, to realize that images of the woman in African literature are diverse rather than uniformly limited, that some of these images are found in works by women, and that in such works the women themselves are often quite explicit in attributing female inequality, or disadvantages, to the "mores of traditional African society" as well as to colonialism. This apparent ignorance of the woman writer and her point of view suggests that as critics we have all, male and female, become the victims of our own collective wish fulfillment. Having determined, for whatever reason, that the African woman does not merit discussion as a serious writer, we have persuaded ourselves that she does not exist as a writer at all.

In fairness to the critics, they are not the only ones who have had some difficulty in grasping or accepting the *idea* of African women writers. One of the writers themselves, Efua Sutherland, is not entirely enthusiastic about being described as a woman writer: "Somehow, I find prescriptions like Women writers very entertaining, and can't manage to respond seriously to it."[2] Quite apart from the oddity of rejecting one prescription (female) while accepting another (African), Sutherland's disclaimer tends to distort or confuse rather than clarify. Her own works as dramatist are dominated by a preoccupation with the experience of women who are, at times, quite forthright in protesting what they see as sexual inequality. These women often insist on their integrity, not only as Africans in specific cultural terms or as human beings in "universal" moral terms, but also as women occupying specific sexual roles. In her odd distaste for being called a woman writer, Sutherland flatly contradicts one of the most obvious concerns of her own work. Even more unfortunately, in the process she lends indirect support, inadvertently or otherwise, to the very tradition that has obscured or ignored the achievements of writers like herself—the critical tradition of pretending or insisting that *women* writers do not exist in Africa, or that, if they do, they are insignificant and generally unworthy of serious critical attention.

It is necessary to belabor the persistence of this traditional neglect because it has had the unfortunate effect of encouraging a perversely respectable kind of ignorance. Since most of us have become accustomed to reading and studying African literature as if it were an exclusive male preserve, we have created a situation in which very few students of the literature seem to be aware that there are women writers in Africa. This kind of institutionalized ignorance seems to be the most likely, and charitable, explanation for oddly distorted claims about the nature of female heroism in the literature.

Such ignorance also leads to another, more complacent view of women in contemporary Africa. With very few people having read, or even heard of, African women writers, it has been relatively easy to perpetuate the image of the free-spirited and independent African woman whose problems, as woman, have flowed from colonialism rather than indigenous mores. This image is bandied from seminar to seminar, and conference to conference, until it has become one of the more enduring clichés of African studies everywhere: "The African woman doesn't need to be liberated because she's already liberated." Or, in the words of Senegal's Léopold Senghor, "Contrary to what is often thought today the African woman doesn't need to be liberated. She has been free for many thousands of years."[3] But the question of need or the idea of freedom may be quite relative, and may not be as easily disposed of as the cliché presupposes. Women writers like Aidoo, Emecheta, Head, and others seem quite unpersuaded that women are free, or have been as free, as Senghor declares. In fact, these women writers repeatedly and vigorously protest sexual inequality in both pre-colonial and postcolonial Africa.

Instead of studying women writers in any significant detail, we have tended to concern ourselves primarily with women as *subjects* in the literature—that is to say, with women as they are viewed by men. For example, Nigeria's Cyprian Ekwensi is well known for his interest in women characters and in the woman's situation in modern (urban) Nigeria. His novel, *Jagua Nana* (1961), has at-tracted considerable attention on this account. In fact Jagua Nana, the heroine of the novel, could be one of the most frequently dis-cussed heroines in contemporary African fiction.[4] In spite of the journalistic sensationalism which so often mars Ekwensi's fiction, there is a certain power in the personality of the woman through whom Ekwensi develops his satire of urban life in Nigeria. For all his satiric realism, Ekwensi's handling of Jagua Nana is ultimately shaped by a certain limited, and limiting, idealism about women and their traditional roles—an idealism that assumes that marriage and motherhood, per se, are unqualified routes to female fulfill-ment and redemption. Thus, after a seedy if sensational life-style in Lagos, Jagua Nana has to be redeemed by her subsequent devotion (albeit short-lived) to motherhood and rural living.

For his part Léopold Senghor's idealistic images of women have attracted favorable attention, especially from Sylvia Washington Bâ: "The eminence of woman as source, channel, and guardian of life force places her in a temporal perspective that transcends the confines of the present."[5]

It is easy to see how Senghor uses women as life-force symbols that transcend death by representing a continuous cycle of birth and renewal. In Senghor's poetry the African woman is a metaphysical symbol of sorts, through whom the poet transcends the confines of death and time. Nevertheless, one needs to ask, as Bâ never does, if this narrow image of womanhood has the effect of allowing us all —artists and critics—to transcend (that is, ignore) the confines of the woman's present (that is, the palpable disadvantages of her day-to-day existence). The fact is that the transcendental ease with which Senghor handles women in his poetry does not come readily, if at all, to women writers. His enthusiastic images of African women are of limited usefulness in the understanding of the woman's actual situation in Africa, because these images are so uniformly, and cloyingly, idealized.

In Senghor's poetry one is not left with a direct confrontation with the realities of the woman's life in African societies, but an idealized picture of African womanhood. This image is important in his works, "Femme Noire" for example, primarily as a symbol of Mother Africa. Senghor's corporate, idealized womanhood has less to do with women as such and much more to do with a certain image of Africa as promised land: Mother Africa is the source of the poet's African sense, and it is the nutrient of that African identity which assumes a certain urgency when the poet's (European) education threatens to weaken his ties with those African roots. This is not necessarily an illegitimate interest in womanhood, but we do need to distinguish it from a more complex and analytical response to women as women.

Nigeria's Chinua Achebe is rare among male writers in that his fiction explicitly draws this kind of distinction. Consequently, the Ibo woman occupies an ambiguous position in his first novel, *Things Fall Apart* (1958). On one hand, she is decidedly subordinate to the men in her society. On the other hand, her society idealizes her as the figure of supreme motherhood. Uchendu, one of the older men in the novel, explains this ambiguity to his nephew Okonkwo, the hero of the novel: "We all know that a man is the head of the family and his wives do his bidding. A child belongs to its father and his family and not to its mother and her family. A man belongs to his fatherland and not to his motherland. And yet we say Nneka—'Mother is Supreme.' Why is that?" Uchendu answers his own question by explaining that the mother's supremacy arises from her archetypal role as protector: she is the one who comforts the child in trouble, and her own homeland, not the father's, is the traditional refuge for any family member who encounters serious problems in adulthood.[6] Taken together, U-chendu's question and answer imply that Achebe is offering an important distinction between an idealized image of womanhood and the subordinate role of the woman in Ibo society, between a mythic concept of supreme motherhood and the limited status of the woman who is required to do her husband's bidding in her day-to-day life.

Ousmane Sembène of Senegal offers an even more unusual male viewpoint. He does not idealize women in the transcendental way that Senghor does. Rather, he goes considerably beyond Achebe's somewhat noncommittal distinction between the idealization of motherhood and the realities of the woman's everyday world. Sembène emphasizes the subordination of women in his society and his harsh social realism focuses on their limited opportunities. This is the kind of emphasis that distinguishes the 1957 novel, *Les Bouts de Bois de Dieu (God's Bits of Wood)*. It describes the birth of the labor union movement in (French) colonial Senegal during the 1940s with women playing significant roles. The novel treats the labor movement itself as part of a broad social phenomenon which will eventually lead to a new and independent nation, one that will facilitate racial and cultural integrity while liberating and respecting its women as full equals: "women became conscious that a change was coming for them as well. . . . And the men began to understand that if the times were bringing forth a new breed of men, they were also bringing forth a new breed of women."[7]

Taken together Senghor, Achebe, and Sembène represent fairly diverse male views of the African woman. Although Senghor represents a majority assumption about African women, as liberated figures, it is still important to recognize the diversity of the views described. This diversity indicates that even among the male authors there is significant variety of opinion regarding the woman's role and experience in Africa. In light of these observable differences it is imperative that students of the literature make an effort to find out what the woman herself has had to say.

Interest in the woman writer in Africa has focused primarily on the white writer—especially those from southern Africa such as Olive Schreiner, Nadine Gordimer, and Doris Lessing. When these writers refer to black women, they do so as outsiders with an even more limited knowledge of the African woman's everyday existence than the black (male) writer's. In the case of Doris Lessing, we are dealing with a writer whose enormous output frequently has nothing to do with Africa. The point is not that these writers are unimportant, or limited, on their own terms. It is that they are not the ones from whom we can reasonably expect to receive a full and informed exploration of the African woman's experience, and, of course, they do not claim to offer one.

Interest shown in the African woman as writer has been spotty. Among the longer, book-length surveys of African literature, only one, O. R. Dathorne's *The Black Mind*, bothers to comment on a few of the women. Given the broad scope of the study, the comments on each writer are necessarily sketchy, and are not able to make up for years of neglect. In some instances, the remarks on a writer are remarkably short-sighted. It is bewildering, for example, to read that Flora Nwapa's heroine, Efuru, in the novel of the same name, is a supernatural being, when the novelist takes great pains to emphasize the mundane, everyday realities of her life as a woman.[8] In other cases there are puzzling omissions. He discusses Grace Ogot's poorly written fiction, but there is no mention of Bessie Head, one of the most ambitious and challenging novelists from southern Africa.

Among the shorter and more specialized studies, Elizabeth Gunner has offered a necessary reminder of the woman's historical contributions to oral literature in Africa. As she points out, Zulu praise poetry customarily included works by women, whose compositions reflected facets of their society that were significant to women.[9] In other words, the voice of the African woman has always been heard in African literature. As far as modern African literature is concerned, Maryse Conde has offered some of the more detailed comments about the theme of womanhood in writings by African women—specifically, Flora Nwapa, Ama Ata Aidoo and Grace Ogot.[10]

Conde takes the writers seriously enough to give them the kind of detailed attention usually withheld by other critics. In the case of Flora Nwapa, the critic illuminates the complex personality of the Nwapa woman and the concrete images of her society, but Conde frequently brings to the text certain political expectations that distort her critical perspective. She commends Nwapa and Aidoo for their social realism, especially for uncompromisingly depicting the disadvantages of their women. However, in the next breath the

critic is chastizing the writers for showing how talented and independent women are often thwarted or destroyed by the male-
dominated societies in which they live. Instead of recognizing this
destruction and waste as the logical effect of a realistic vision,
Conde blames it all on the writers, complaining that they destroy
the gifted females that they create. This kind of complaint is political
wish fulfillment rather than responsible or insightful criticism.
Conde is complaining that the writers have refused to transcend
their social reality by offering an easy, idealized vision of a purely
hypothetical equality. In any event, it is quite misleading to argue,
as Conde does, that all the women whom these writers create are
destroyed or wasted. The critic's ideal of social equality or female
independence ought not to distort or obscure the degree to which a
writer, any writer, succeeds in depicting the less than ideal lives of
women. However much one may be inclined to agree with Conde's
negative views of Grace Ogot's skills as a writer, one also suspects
that the critic fails to detect some substantial ambiguities in Ogot's
social vision because she starts off with the impression that Ogot
lacks a "liberated" point of view. In other words, Conde seems to
assume that an uncompromising realism is incompatible with a
thorough-going commitment to the ideal of women's equality.

Femi Ojo-Ade's rather intemperate and short-sighted overview
of Bessie Head's fiction presents us with the opposite problem:
"Once the notion of women's liberation is erased from the critic's
mind, he can settle down to a fruitful examination of women in
Head's three novels."[11] It is never clear what the critic understands,
or means, by the term "women's liberation." It is even less clear
how one can discuss the situation of women in Head's work without dealing with the issue of women's liberation in even the broadest
sense—as a preoccupation with the moral and political ideals of
woman's equality and female individuality. Very few African
writers, male or female, are as explicit as Bessie Head in raising
these issues, and to ignore them is simply to ignore the very heart
of her fiction. Ojo-Ade manages to do this—largely, it appears,
because the critic's difficulty with the idea of women's liberation
does not allow for a thorough "examination of women" in the
novelist's works.

All of this inevitably raises the issue of relevance. How relevant is the issue of women's liberation, which we normally understand as a Western political preoccupation, to the study of African women writers? Clearly, the specific political goals of women's liberation movements vary in the West itself, even within single countries like the United States. Considered in its broadest sense, women's liberation is concerned with issues of female identity. However much the specific issues and attending definitions may vary from society to society and from culture to culture, the broad problem of female identity and inequality, in relation to male dominance, remains constant. Donald Bayer Burness recognizes this in his brief discussion of sexual identity in Aidoo's short stories. If there is a shortcoming in this aspect of his study, it is its tunnel vision—the narrow and erroneous assumption that Aidoo's exclusive emphasis on African womanhood makes her unique in African literature.[12]

There is one other significant failing in the Burness study. The summary of Aidoo's sexual themes, the most obvious of them at any rate, is generally satisfactory, but the short shrift paid to Aidoo's skills as a short-story writer is disconcerting. A careful study of her art is unlikely to conclude, as Burness does, that she has failed to master the short-story form. Aidoo is one of the more impressive short-story writers on the continent—not only because her themes of womanhood are realistically conceived and stated, but also because her work reflects careful attention to the integration of theme and form. Unfortunately, Burness' short-sightedness in this regard is typical of a general shortcoming in the handful of studies that have appeared on African women writers. There is a tendency to approach these writers with an almost exclusive emphasis on social and political statements. The critics have treated the writers as if the novels, plays, short stories, and poems are simply political tracts, or anthropological studies. In so doing they ignore the extent to which such works should be approached as committed works of art in which theme, or social vision, is integrated with an effective sense of design and language.

The present study seeks to remedy this shortcoming by demonstrating the manner in which all the major women writers contribute to African literature, not only by voicing the woman's view as such, but also by the manner in which that view, whatever its nature, is integrated with the writer's art. Consequently, writers like Aidoo, Sutherland, and Nwapa have made distinctive contributions to the genres in which they work—Aidoo in the short story, Sutherland in the theater, and Nwapa in the novel. They have managed to develop their themes in such a way that their chosen forms are inseparable from the manner in which they perceive women and society in general. Nwapa's novels depend on a narrative form rooted in the oral modes of everyday village life, and, in turn, those oral forms are intrinsic to every detail of the woman's life. Aidoo utilizes a variety of short-story forms that vary from adapted oral techniques to adapted Western forms. In each case, the selected form reflects the experience of the woman. Finally, Sutherland's drama repeatedly develops analogies between the role-playing of the theater and (sexual) role-playing in society.

But in concentrating on the achievements of the major writers this study tries to avoid being unduly restrictive. It seeks to offer a broad survey of women writers in African literature, for most of these writers are preoccupied with sexual roles and identity in one way or another, even if the artistic achievements are uneven. This preoccupation ranges from the indirect statements of some writers to the direct protests of others. They are all the other voices of African literature, and the present study seeks to draw attention both to what they say, and to how they express themselves.

2 The Woman's Voice in African Literature

The contributions of women to African literature have not been limited to the modern period. Women have always played a considerable role, as storytellers and performers, in the oral tradition. The tradition always had a significant place for the voice of the woman singing or reciting tales from her own perspective as wife, mother, and housekeeper. This is the kind of perspective that is heard in the mocking ribaldry of an Amharic song from Ethiopia. The song ridicules the man as "Trousers of wind and buttons of hail/A horse of mist and a swollen ford."[1]

In some communities, the woman as oral artist has been known to voice her society's experiences as a whole. In South Africa, for example, the late A. C. Jordan depended largely on older women who were renowned storytellers when he set out to compile his collection of Xhosa tales. The dominance of women in the oral traditions explored by Jordan moved one commentator to note the contrasting situation in modern South Africa where there has been a "total disappearance of women from the literary scene" because colonialism, Western technology, and literacy have diminished the importance of the oral tradition in which the woman artist formerly flourished.[2] Women artists have not totally disappeared from the literary scene in contemporary Africa as a whole. It is undeniable that, compared with their male counterparts, they have remained a rather small handful, but they have contributed to some standard themes which have become the regular staple of writer and critic alike in modern African literature.

For example, the poetry of Aquah Laluah (Gladys Casely-Hayford) of Ghana explores the familiar tensions between Africa and the West. Poems like "Nativity" examine the conflicitng claims of Christianity and African identity by re-creating the nativity scene with an African cast. The work suffers from trite, derivative language ("Within a native hut, ere stirred the dawn") that reflects Laluah's severe limitations as a poet and her ready acceptance of derogatory Western terms like "native." In spite of its severe artistic limitations, the poem as a whole is interesting because, conventional Christian that she is, the poet still feels constrained to modify the white, European images of Christian myth in order to accommodate a persistent sense of being African. Here, too, the sexual issue is not far beneath the surface. The "Africanization" of the nativity scene is fraught with sexual significance, for it is not only unconventionally black, it is also sexually integrated to an unconventional degree. The (African) Virgin Mary and the black Christ child are visited by women as well as by men: "Black women brought their love so wise/And kissed their motherhood into His mother's eyes."[3]

In Uganda, Barbara Kimenye offers a sustained, satiric view of these cultural conflicts. Her two major collections of short stories are set in a Ugandan village, and they depict the family lives, private feuds, and public troublemakers of the community. Kimenye suffers from a marked tendency to patronize her characters by way of caricature, but she does deserve credit for a very rare attempt, in contemporary African literature, to use satiric comedy in a sustained way in her two collections, *Kalasanda* (1965), and *Kalasanda Revisited* (1966).

The central focus in each collection, one that links all the characters and the stories, is the village of Kalasanda. Characters recur from one story to another—the Christian leaders, the chief, the owner of the Happy Bar, and Nantondo the old village gossip. In the process they lend a collective or composite personality to the village itself. It is a fairly conservative village with a deep-rooted sense of its own past—one that does not take kindly, for example, to an abortive attempt by the Christians to destroy the sacred tree which goes back to the indigenous religious past. The village is also receptive to change, as long as that change is tempered—as it is in the person of Chief Musizi—with respect for the local traditions.

Like Aquah Laluah, Kimenye makes us aware of the woman's presence in this hybrid world of old and new, indigenous and alien systems. While Laluah's "Nativity" does this within a Christian setting, she manages, as we have seen, to offer a fairly subdued but pointed criticism of the white male perspective that dominates Christian mythology. Kimenye's comedy deals much more conventionally with women than Laluah's work does. Women appear in a variety of roles in Kalasanda village life. There are prominent wives of community leaders, and the Christians who fail ignominously in their assault on the sacred tree are a generally formidable group of women. The Happy Bar is operated by a woman. Finally, the most dominant character in both collections is the widow Nantondo, an irrepressible gossip and general troublemaker.

Despite the prominence of women characters in her work, Kimenye's handling of such characters is decidedly more limited, and limiting, than even Aquah Laluah's Christian restraint. Kimenye's patronizing caricatures make her characters, men and women, one-dimensional objects of ridicule rather than complex and credible personalities. In the case of the women this kind of caricature usually depends on well-known, derogatory stereotypes of women. In *Kalasanda Revisited*, for example, the Christian women are absurd, not because of their Christian fanaticism as such and their comical disdain for the local past—although these are clearly factors in the story—but because they are really hysterical women. As such, they are unbalanced, and silly enough to attack a tree in the dead of night with machetes—reaping their just reward when they are attacked by a swarm of ants.[4]

In *Kalasanda*, the unexpected visit of a local dignitary, the Kabaka, triggers the usual bustle and frenzy in the small, self-important village. It is the women who are prone to be hysterical: the president of the Mother's Union becomes a bustling busybody "in the thick of things," and when the inevitable tensions arise between families and friends vying for the Kabaka's attention, "sides were taken with the swiftness peculiar to the female species at moments like this."[5] The basic problem in stories like these is not that Kimenye attributes certain traits to women, but that she does so by implying, rather stereotypically, that these traits are somehow intrinsically and endemically female. In the process she makes no attempt to question the source of these traits and their links with how women are traditionally treated and perceived in their communities. This is the failing that reduces her female characters to mere stereotypes and caricatures, and in the process, distinguishes her work from more substantial writers like Buchi Emecheta or Flora Nwapa when the latter describe conventional female failings.

This explains the limited range of the Kimenye woman. She is hysterical, or in stories like "The Winner" she is a scheming manipulator. This story describes the comical dilemma of a man who is suddenly besieged by friends, relatives, and strangers after he wins money in a public lottery (football pools). It is a woman, his cousin Sarah, who emerges as the real winner in all of this because she successfully persuades the man, Pius, that he really needs her to help him keep house (and spend his money) now that he is wealthy (*Kalasanda*, pp. 37-48). Finally, there is the widow Nantondo who is both schemer and hysterical female. She is forever the gossip and the troublemaker, with all the manners and looks of a comically evil witch: "grizzled whiskers," "thousands of tiny, dry wrinkles," "shaven head," and "scrawny neck" (*Kalasanda*, p. 8). In the Nantondo character, Kimenye's approach to women is seen in its most obvious but generally representative sense; the woman is a generally amusing stereotype. That is as far as Kimenye's limited caricature goes—or seems capable of going.

The subject of cultural conflict and change receives more thought-provoking and substantial treatment from another comic prose writer. Adaora Lily Ulasi (Nigeria) dramatizes the impact of the colonial system on the fabric of traditional Ibo society in her two novels, *Many Thing You No Understand* (1970) and *Many Thing Begin For Change* (1971), with a deft interweaving of the tragic and the satiric. The second novel is a sequel to the first because both works describe the dramatic unfolding of a single series of events. When the village chief of Ukana dies he is buried, according to custom, with the heads of twenty of his subjects. This triggers the main conflict that forms the basis of Ulasi's plot. Head-hunting is sanctioned by local custom, but from the viewpoint of the British colonizer it is clearly murder. At least this is the firm conviction of John McIntosh, the young assistant district officer for the area.

McIntosh's efforts to track down the head-hunters are thwarted from two directions. On one hand, the new chief, Obieze, is a wily man whose supporters hide the head-hunters from the reach of the colonial police, and he takes steps—including witchcraft—to make sure that a potential eyewitness of the head-hunting (a brother of one victim) is too intimidated to give evidence. On the other hand, McIntosh's immediate superior, District Officer Mason, discourages his zealous young assistant. A ruthlessly efficient administrator whenever the occasion demands it, the veteran district officer is reluctant to interfere with local customs, unless there is a clear threat to the (colonial) peace, or the offence is so flagrantly public that it would be impossible, and imprudent, for the colonial administration to ignore it. In the absence of witnesses, he is inclined to let this matter rest as one of rumor and local custom, rather than one of criminal importance.

Before illness forces McIntosh to return to England, his investigations establish that a crime has been committed. There is no proof of the head-hunters' actual identity, or of the new chief's complicity. McIntosh's sudden and mysterious illness—allegedly the result of witchcraft—prevents him from finding such proof. Now that the fact of the crime has actually been established, Mason can no longer ignore the matter. He takes up the investigation after McIntosh leaves, but when he gets too close to the truth he is lured into an ambush and killed by Obieze and his men.

From here the chain reaction of events continues to its climax in the second novel, *Many Thing Begin For Change*. The work is a highly dramatic account of the prolonged cat-and-mouse game between Obieze and George Hughes, the district commissioner, who has been forced into the picture by the mysterious disappearance of his district officer. Chief Obieze loses the game in the end. The commissioner lacks the hard evidence to arrest the chief for complicity in the head-hunting and in Mason's murder, but he manages to convey the opposite impression. Rather than submit to the disgrace of what he fears to be impending arrest, Obieze commits suicide.

Both novels are well written. Ulasi has a considerable knack for building and sustaining narrative suspense, not only through plot construction, but through deft handling of characters and personal motives. The accumulation of events centers on the slow but inexorable implication of Obieze and on the subtle, political skills of colonial administration. Because of this, Ulasi's narrative is a finely controlled study in human nature. The investigation does not develop on the basis of hard facts and demonstrable assumptions, but on the basis of suspicions and prejudices on both sides. This is where Ulasi's tragicomic handling of cultural conflicts is integrated with a certain interest in sexual roles.

The intrigues and investigations are not simply reflections of cultural conflict—local custom versus British law—as such, though this is undoubtedly the central issue. They are also interwoven with the patterns of masculine role-playing which seem integral to the nature and significance of political power in a male-oriented world. In fact, Ulasi generally tempers the emphasis on cultural conflict by ironically underscoring the degree to which the opponents on both sides of the cultural barrier share very similar attitudes toward the relationship between sex and power. On the African side, Chief Obieze and his men are unquestioned figures of authority. The exercise of such power is not only a social and political function, it is also a self-consciously *masculine* process. As one of the headhunters makes clear in previewing the rule of the new chief, political stability will depend on the extent to which certain women in the community are made to stay in their (nonpolitical) places. From his point of view, the exercise of power, or an overt interest in the subject, is unseemly in a woman. The new chief's mother is a very bad woman for this reason. She shows all the signs of a woman who is prone to political meddling. Such a woman is not a real woman at all, she is something of a freak because she is attempting to usurp a masculine role: "And she get hair for chest. Any woman way get hair for chest no good at all!"[6]

On the British side, Maurice Mason's strength and effectiveness as a district officer stems from the same kind of masculine ego which underlies his sexual relationships. His wife lives in England, and he has not visited her in years. He prefers sexual affairs with African women; since any kind of involvement with *them* is out of the question, he can remain securely detached—and in control—in these affairs. This is the same kind of manipulative detachment that marks his exercise of administrative power. Conversely, young McIntosh is a well-meaning but ineffective administrator. He is too sensitive, especially to the emotional implications of local customs like head-hunting, and he is much too susceptible to emotional involvement, with his African servant for one, who promptly betrays him by passing on confidential administrative matters and information to Chief Obieze. McIntosh lacks that capacity for a frankly self-centered masculinity which one finds in Obieze, Mason, and District Commissioner George Hughes. It is noteworthy, in this regard, that McIntosh is also sexually repressed and quite removed from the heterosexual ebullience of men like Obieze and Mason. His only sexual activity or interest takes the form of a limited, and necessarily furtive, homosexual affair with his servant.

Ulasi's women have a slyly subversive response to all of this. There is a certain kind of ego, "a little boy," in every man, Chief Obieze's wife observes to herself in *Many Thing Begin for Change*.[7] In other words, the colonial context as a whole is really a large-scale exercise in various patterns of holding and using power. As such, colonialism demonstrates the way in which its (male) power-brokers perceive and value power—irrespective of whether they are colonizers or colonial subjects. There is an intense egotism in the perception and exercise of power. It is the kind of egotism that makes for abrasive, unpleasantly manipulative personalities, but without it, one is ineffective in the brutal realities of political and social dominance in the world in general and in colonial societies in particular. Finally, men seem quite adept at this kind of power-brokerage because so many societies are male-dominated and therefore encourage men to retain a certain boyish fascination with the games of power—the kind of egotistical fascination that is, ironically, necessary for the effective exercise of power.

Given her frank interest in the significance of sexual roles in the colonial process, Ulasi is a bridge of sorts between those women writers who concentrate primarily on the broad issues of cultural conflict and those who are more immediately interested in the significance of sexual roles. The latter develop their themes almost exclusively from the perspective of women, and they do this by emphasizing how women perceive their society and their own roles in that society. I must emphasize at this point that I am not attributing to these writers some *inherent* and universally female viewpoint which is invariably incompatible with some male (African) world view. Attributions of this kind are often more notable for creating endless and unproductive debate than for shedding really useful light on the literature itself.

What I am suggesting is that in writing about women and their men, these writers emphasize that the experience, identity, and role of a woman are all distinguishable from a man's, in culturally definable terms; that there is a greater preoccupation among these women writers with what they conceive to be the limited roles of women; and that on these counts such women have produced a body of literature that is distinguishable from the male mainstream, which is often the only presumed subject whenever we think or write about African literature.

For example, male writers like Ekwensi and Senghor automatically define ideal womanhood in terms of motherhood, and the men in Achebe's fiction subscribe to a prevailing and idealistic notion of supreme motherhood, but the women writers discussed here are usually ambivalent toward motherhood. They seldom see it in terms of an absolutely sacrosanct mystique. Of course, they usually recognize the importance and the enormous prestige of the maternal role in the lives of most women in heavily child-oriented societies, and the writers can hardly be described as anti-motherhood. They do raise serious questions about the manner in which the mystique of motherhood creates limitations for some women by imposing restrictions on their sense of choice: they are expected to be mothers, several times over, and if they do not measure up to the community's expectations, by choice or by natural necessity, then they must bear with the stigma of being regarded as less than whole women.

A brief comparison between two novels, one written by a man and the other by a woman, is helpful. Elechi Amadi's *The Concubine* (1966) and Flora Nwapa's *Efuru* (1966) are both Nigerian novels about Ibo women who do not have successful relationships with men. Amadi's Ihuoma is loved by the jealous Sea King, and Nwapa's Efuru has been chosen by the Woman of the Lake to be her special worshipper. In each case, the deity represents the separateness and special character of the woman involved. In Amadi's novel the situation is really a male problem. That is, the Sea King's love for Ihuoma makes her unavailable to mortal men. Consequently a succession of infatuated men lose property, limbs, and lives in determined but futile attempts to bed and/or wed Ihuoma. In Nwapa's work the emphasis is not the male's desire or need but the woman's, Efuru's, needs. The Woman of the Lake is really a divine symbol of Efuru's sense of self as an unusual woman, one who cannot tolerate male egocentricity well enough to be the conventional wife. Efuru's eventual decision to devote herself to being the deity's special worshipper signifies her acceptance of her own attitudes as a woman.

Amadi's novel is not necessarily inferior because it reflects a predominantly male interest in the woman's role and accessibility. Indeed, narrative logic and realism would demand that this be the prevailing interest in a novel that examines relationships between men and women in a male-dominated society, but, and this is the crucial issue here, the converse is true of those female-oriented perspectives naturally expected from the woman writer. The real issue is that the very existence of clearly demarcated sexual roles in some African societies has left room for those women writers who have chosen to elaborate upon the woman's perception of her own role. As a consequence, these women writers are much more involved with those aspects of the woman's experience which do not depend on the man's perception of his needs, but are based on the woman's awareness of hers. This kind of involvement is most explicit in the works of protest writers.

Drawing distinctions between protest writers and serious artists is often risky, sometimes mischievous. Such distinctions tend to inspire all the well known, shopworn clichés about art versus protest. In distinguishing between women as protest writers and other women in African literature, I do not intend to imply that protest is limited to a separate group of women whose works are inferior to, and less significant than, the writings of others. Major writers like Aidoo and Head are often quite direct in their protest, and the presence of protest elements has not compromised the complexity of their art. Conversely, I do not wish to suggest that some writers should be treated as major artists simply because we happen to sympathize with the burden of their protest. But after all of these pre-cautionary notes, we still need to emphasize the importance of a group of writers—protest writers—whose artistic merit is limited but whose blunt and frequently persuasive charges of sexual in-equality offer their readers direct insights into the African woman's perception of herself and her society.

These insights encompass a fairly wide range of concerns from the subject of poverty to the everyday chores of motherhood and the inescapable drudgery of rural life in poorer communities. In these works the protester's directness and undisguised passion com-plement the oblique and complex statements of the major artists. The protester's straightforwardness is especially helpful in the study of women's literature in Africa because their vehemence is in itself significant. It challenges the entrenched image of African women as already liberated persons. With all of their artistic fail-ings the protest writers occupy a special place in the literature: they voice a passionate sense of grievance that compels the attention of anyone who seriously undertakes an examination of the ways in which African women view their lives in contemporary Africa.

This tradition of protest goes back to some of the earlier English-language literature of modern West Africa. In her best known short story, Adelaide Casely-Hayford (Sierra Leone) describes a conflict of generations between Mista Courifer (after whom the story is named) and his son Tomas, who rebels against his father's servile reverence for the religion and social customs of the British colonizer. Although Tomas has rediscovered the Wolof dress and the ethnic pride his father had taught him to despise, he also rebels against the traditional male dominance in his culture. As much as he dislikes the English and most of their customs, he prefers the way in which Englishmen treat their wives: Englishmen eat with their wives but African men in his culture eat "the best of everything" while dining alone, then leave the left-overs for the children, and for the wives who had been "slaving away in the kitchen" to prepare the meal.[8]

In a later generation of writers Mabel Dove-Danquah (Ghana), the first woman to be elected to a government assembly in modern Africa, reflects a certain distaste for traditional sexual roles. Her short story, "Anticipation," is a sardonic account of polygamy and male arrogance. An aging chief impetuously marries a beautiful dancer, at first sight, only to discover on his wedding night that he had already married her two years before—but had lost all trace and memory of her among thirty-nine other wives.[9]

Mozambique's Noemia de Sousa writes out of bitter rebellion against Portuguese colonial rule. In the poem "Appeal" the satire is savagely double-edged. First, the poem evokes that transcendental image of motherhood which men often cherish. Then it contrasts that image ("heroic sister") with a somber reality: her "sister" has a "strangled" and "tired" voice, and she is a servile figure, "leashed with children and submission." Second, the attack on sexual subordination is intensified by a scathing parallel. The "mean and brutal rhino-whip" of the European colonizer has lashed the African woman—in other words, sexual subordination at the hands of her own men and colonial subjugation by the European outsider have become interchangeable in the life of the African woman. In a male-oriented, colonial society she suffers the double disadvantage of being African and female.[10]

Kenya's Marina Gashe (Elimo Njaw) relies on images of drudgery to portray rural women as beasts of burden. In the poem, "The Village," old women and young wives work like "Donkeys," all "Stirring up the soil . . . Like chickens looking for worms." Here, and in de Sousa's poem, the pointed emphasis on the burdens of womanhood is explicit. It rejects the idealistic notion of motherhood per se as an unequivocal, transfiguring triumph for the woman. Consequently, Gashe's women are bowed down under "loads on their backs/And babies tied to their bellies."[11]

Neither de Sousa nor Gashe attack the role of motherhood as such, but they clearly set out to de-romanticize the image of motherhood. In much the same way, Medard Kasese (Zambia) portrays the hardships of some mothers in the poem, "Black Mother." The husbands of Kasese's mothers are insensitive, turning their backs during labor pains and snoring during the long hours of night-nursing. In turn, the children grow up to neglect the mother when she is old.[12] Kasese's "Black Mother" is worlds apart from Léopold Senghor's "Black Woman ("Femme Noire"). Kasese's snoring husband has his counterpart in the satiric poem, "Wife of the Husband," by Kenya's Micere Githae-Mugo. This work indicts the insensitivity and the privileged ease which the male has arrogated to himself. At night he protects the family hut with "snores," but when day returns the real burdens and responsibilities fall on the woman's shoulders. Those burdens "weigh heavily over/the stooping mother as she/sweeps the hut."[13] The trite language notwithstanding, Githae-Mugo and other poets like her seem fairly unanimous in imputing an *outsider's* image to the man, even as they debunk the traditionally male idealization of motherhood. In fact, Gashe's "The Village" ends with a suggestive reference to the absent male. He rides away to his own business at dawn, so that the village is really the woman's world—a world of drudgery.

The man's departure also dramatizes the kind of separation that is inherent in a strongly defined, rigidly maintained pattern of sexual roles. The "village of toil" in Gashe's work is the woman's world. The vagueness of that world into which the man rides at dawn reflects his own distance from her world—just as much as it represents the woman's distance from, and ignorance of, his world. The woman's temptation, some may even say her need, is to bring down the barriers between these separate worlds. This is the kind of revolutionary change that Francesca Yetunde Pereira (Nigeria) contemplates in "Two Strange Worlds." Her language is as clumsy as that of the other minor protest poets, but here too the poem voices a significant restiveness about traditional sexual roles. She complains that women who attempt to invade the alien world of men are fools if they try to do so while "manifesting/Weakness in tenderness."[14]

Pereira does not condemn the invasion itself as folly. She does question the foolhardiness of attempting to function in the relatively strange world of men (as, increasingly, women must do in modern, Westernized Africa) with the perceptions and emotional responses that have been shaped and defined exclusively in the woman's world—a world that is as strange to the man as his is to her. In effect, the poet is demanding that there be a reassessment of old role definitions which are based on the continuation of two strange (that is, incompatible) worlds. In so doing she implies that there is a need for the kind of social changes that will enable men and women to live together in a single and fully integrated world.

The differences between male and female experiences or perspectives also attract writers outside the tradition of overt protest. Kenya's Grace Ogot is a good example of these minor writers whose protest is subdued or indirect—especially when we consider her novel *The Promised Land* (1966) and her collection of short stories *Land Without Thunder* (1968).[15] Generally speaking, Ogot avoids direct protest. Sexual roles and attitudes are described with little or no narrative commentary or political judgment. The kind of subtlety or multiple suggestiveness normally associated with this kind of narrative technique is not particularly evident in Ogot's work, and this is largely due to Ogot's limitations as a fiction writer. She relies on an uninspired, rather pedestrian style, and her characters are usually too wooden or underdeveloped to be capable of convincing emotional responses.

Ogot's *Promised Land* is a melodramatic tale of tribal hatreds in Tanzania (Tanganyika) where Ochola and his wife Nyapol have settled as farmers after migrating from Kenya. As members of the Luo tribe, their success and wealth provoke the envy of the locals. Ochola's neighbor, a witch-doctor, is the most envious and malignant of the lot and he casts a spell on Ochola. The latter falls ill and is eventually cured by a healer, but he and Nyapol have to abandon their farm and their wealth in order to return to Kenya before their enemy can endanger their lives again.

The couple are sexual archetypes. Ochola is the conventionally masculine figure—dominant and jealous of his male prerogatives as head of the family. His material ambition and his underlying fear of failure are partly attributed to the poverty from which he comes; but these traits are also linked with his masculine sense of self. In fact, his ambition emerges as an ambiguous quality in the novel. It leads to material success, but at the price of severing important ties with their community and family in Kenya. In the end he literally has to be dragged away from his farm because, ambitious and greedy as he is, he is willing to expose himself and his family to further danger rather than give up his wealth. On the other hand, Nyapol is the model of the traditional wife— obedient, subservient to her husband, and performing without question all the duties that custom has assigned to women only.

There is an implied judgment underlying all of this. As a woman, Nyapol has been spared the kind of aggressive ego which fuels her husband's obsessively materialistic ambition. She is as depressed by poverty as he is, but is much less willing to seek material wealth at the cost of family and community ties. On this basis, her female role seems to facilitate a certain humaneness that counterbalances her husband's materialism. It also has its own strength. Unlike her husband, for example, she is not afraid to show that she is fearful of things—like a strange society, or the night noises of the forest near their farm. This candor is a kind of strength which he lacks—a moral strength. Moreover, her commitment to family and community not only makes her reluctant to migrate to Tanzania, but is also vindicated in the end when Ochola is forced to return home. Finally, this female humaneness is shared with the spirit of Ochola's dead mother. Her spirit clearly disapproves of his move to Tanzania, and in this regard it is associated with the larger, collective spirit of family and community which Ochola ignores at his peril.

This humaneness is not exclusively, or even inherently, female. Ochola's father, an old man now, also invokes that sense of community and family to which Nyapol appeals. Since Ochola belongs to a new breed of aggressive young men who are determined to acquire wealth at all costs, the clear implication is that the masculine ego has been easily attracted by a new materialism, one that appeals to the young man's need to succeed at the cost of established custom and family ties. Significantly, this new materialism leaves women like Nyapol, and old men like Ochola's father, relatively unmoved.

On the whole, Nyapol is more humane and spiritual than Ochola; her relatively protected and restricted role as a woman shelters her from the success ethic of the masculine world, and from the new, disruptive materialism that produces that ethic. Being more sheltered she is also more traditional, she remains more in touch with her community's cherished spiritual values. This leads to a basic problem in her character and situation, for it is this traditionalism that also ensures her subordination to a palpably limited man. The problem is never resolved in the novel. Nyapol's perspectives prevail to the extent that at the end Ochola is forced to return home. However, he returns under duress, not out of any respect for her wishes or fears, and their relationship remains fairly unchanged. Since neither show any indication that they would have it otherwise, this lack of change is a fairly realistic representation of Nyapol's world. Ogot therefore deserves credit for not imposing some transcendentally liberated or independent image on Nyapol. At the same time, one senses a certain kind of irresolution in the narrative itself—as if the novelist herself is caught between two conflicting responses to Nyapol's traditional world. She recognizes the limiting effects on the woman while emphasizing the spiritual and communal heritage of that traditionalism. The novel stops abruptly— as does so much of Ogot's work—instead of coming to a finished conclusion, and one is left without any kind of implicit or overt narrative judgment on Nyapol's total experience.

There is a similar kind of narrative irresolution in the handling of the Western woman in the novel. Mrs. Thomson is the wife of the white doctor who fails to cure Ochola. She is assertive and independent in her relationship with her husband, and she contrasts these qualities with the docility of local women (p. 175). If Mrs. Thomson's independence contrasts with Nyapol's submissiveness, she is also, as a white Christian, one whose culture and religion make her the perpetual outsider with severely limited relevance to Nyapol's world. Her individuality therefore emerges in the novel as an attractive but alien quality.

This kind of dilemma on Ogot's part continues in her short stories dealing with women—but with a pronounced air of resignation. The African woman chooses the world of the white woman in "The Old White Witch," but the choice really solves nothing. The story describes a strike by the African nurses at a hospital, in defiance of their white matron (the "old white witch"), because they will not empty bedpans as they have been ordered to do. The strike is sparked by the women's strong traditionalism: emptying bedpans will make them ineligible for husbands. Their gesture goes to the heart of Ogot's dilemma. The women unquestioningly accept established sexual codes, including the ones which regulate even the way in which they may earn a living; and at the same time they are, in effect, upholding the integrity of their total cultural tradition out of which those codes have arisen. Indeed this strong sense of cultural integrity baffles Matron Jack who finds that these women are more strong-willed in dealing with her than they are with their own men. In fact, the matron wishes that they were as obedient with her as the men have been (*Land Without Thunder*, p. 17). The point that

Matron Jack, the outsider, misses is that there is no real contradiction between the women's submissiveness to the men and their
resistance to her. In resisting her demands they are fiercely protecting those sexual conventions which they cherish in their own
lives—and which require their submission to men. Ogot's dilemma
consists of the fact that the cultural traditions sanctioning these
sexual conventions are important, almost sacrosanct, in the large
sense of African history and identity. In none of her works are her
women able to reject the conventions while maintaining and cherish-
ing the large cultural tradition—and there is nothing in these works
to suggest that Ogot herself envisions any way in which this could
be done.

The nurse who chooses the world of the white woman takes a
tentative, but eventually ambiguous step in this direction. She is
Monica Adhiambo, Matron Jack's favorite nurse, the one who
actually leads the strike. Monica eventually returns to the hospital
as a patient dying from a stomach infection. The matron nurses her
day and night until the young nurse dies. Since Monica accepts the
Holy Sacrament on her death bed, she has effectively returned to
Matron Jack's Western, Christian values, and, presumably, rejected
the sexual conventions and those broad cultural traditions that led
to the strike. However, if Monica's conversion to the matron's
world represents some kind of triumph over the African tradition
and its sexual codes, it also involves a kind of cultural apostasy. On
this basis, it typifies the unresolved dilemma that baffles Ogot as
much as it does her women.

In fairness to Ogot, we do need to repeat the point made apropos
of a similar dilemma in *The Promised Land*. However much this
may indicate some irresolution on the author's part, it also constitutes a certain kind of realism in her fiction—including the short
stories. The lack of resolutions is also the consequence of continuing, perhaps unresolvable, conflicts and dilemmas in the world
of Ogot's women. In the other short stories which focus on women
this absence of resolutions, or failure of resolutions, effectively
creates an air of resignation, one that barely salvages a poorly
written collection of stories. The women, and the men in their
world, are limited—the men by the familiar patterns of male egotism, and the women by their subordinate status as well as by the

submissiveness shaped by that subordination. The air of resignation with which these limitations are described generally creates the impression that these limitations are a continuing and deeply rooted reality.

In "The Bamboo Hut" the wife of a village chief gives birth to twins, a boy and a girl, but gives the girl away in order to appease the chief's desire for sons only. Years later she has to reveal the deception in order to avert an impending marriage between her son and a strange young woman whom she recognizes as the prospective bridegroom's twin sister. The story simply ends with the chief magnanimously forgiving his wife (pp. 27-37).

"The White Veil" is an even gloomier picture of female duplicity responding to male arrogance and insensitivity. Achola has been jilted for another woman by her fiance Owila because Achola will not go to bed with him before the wedding. He cannot understand why they must forego premarital sex on Christian grounds when their white fellow Christians do not make that kind of sacrifice. When Owila's wedding date has been set, Achola goes to the church, disguised in a white veil, and substitutes herself for the intended bride. She does not reveal her real identity until after the priest has pronounced them married. The story ends with her tearful justification of the deception: Owila is hers because she has loved him all her life, and now he'll always be hers (pp. 111-40). The protestation of love becomes a ringing declaration of life-long vengeance.

While "The White Veil" exposes the duplicity and narrow selfishness in both the man and the woman, the decidedly grim "Elizabeth" emphasizes the woman as victim. Elizabeth is a young typist in the city. She is raped by her male employer, and when she discovers that she is pregnant she commits suicide in front of his house. Apart from Elizabeth's tragic victimization nothing happens in the story. There is no punishment for the man, or even the likelihood of one. We are left with a pious declaration by one of Elizabeth's older women friends: man has defied the laws of society; God alone with deal with him (pp. 189-204).

This kind of passive piety is appropriate in Ogot's fiction because nothing really changes in her world, nor is there any sign of possible change, or even of individual capacity for change. Her men and women are locked into age-old attitudes that are demonstrably limiting and palpably destructive. No one seems able to break away, not even Monica in "The Old White Witch," without undermining and betraying the vital and important cultural traditions with which those attitudes seem to be inextricably intertwined. In one sense, the persistence of the status quo in Ogot's fiction reflects a possible, satiric realism about the persistence of human behavior, especially sexual attitudes, and the basic continuity of human nature. Alternatives, such as they are, are in the hands of God. In another sense the apparent resignation of Ogot's fiction could imply a limitation of some sort. A more imaginative and complex artist, like South Africa's Bessie Head, is quite capable, without a great deal of effort, of emphasizing the continuity of limited social realities while hinting at or envisioning acceptable alternatives within or outside her characters. Indeed she manages to underscore the tenacity of the status quo by the very act of envisioning or attempting to realize such alternatives. It is not possible to find this kind of complexity in Ogot. It is not clear whether she lacks that kind of imaginative breadth or vision, or whether it is simply that her thin narrative style is unable to sustain anything more than the bare-boned, one-dimensional reality of her fictive vision.

On the other hand, Ghana's Patience Henaku Addo is clearly capable of a more complex perception of people and society. Her play, *Company Pot* (1972), examines the experiences of the young urban woman against a background that is almost universal in African literature—the conflicts between an established rural morality and the disturbing, unsettled life styles of the modern, Westernized city.[16] In Addo's play the conflicts center on the attempts of a young woman to win independence from an overly protective rural mother while guarding her integrity and freedom from the attentive men of the big city. She manages to fend off the advances of Pamonie, a small-time racketeer, while gradually winning the affection and respect of the student, Lovelace, who admires her spirit and independent personality. At the play's conclusion Pamonie is conveniently removed from the scene (he is arrested for diamond smuggling), and it appears to Lovelace that he will be rewarded, by way of marriage, for having recognized and respected Akyebi's integrity.

Throughout all of the play Akyebi is increasingly aware of how much her life as woman is based on sexually defined roles. Her female identity brings with it certain predefined sexual rules about what she may or may not do—rules that do not apply to the sexually unrestricted world of men. She discovers that if the city offers her some measure of freedom from the restrictive conventions of rural morality, it also makes her more vulnerable, as a woman, to male exploitiveness in a frankly masculine world—particularly in that part of the world (the modern city) where the protective old rules no longer apply.

Young Akyebi's experience and growth pinpoint a fundamental dilemma in the lives of contemporary women in Africa, one that is analogous to the dilemma with which Ogot wrestles so inconclusively in her fiction: if women choose to remain loyal to and surrounded by the older traditions represented by village life, they will be protected but they will also be restricted in much the same way that Akyebi's mother is restricted. On the other hand, the liberation of the Westernized city and its alien life-style bring their own peculiar perils to the woman who prizes both a sense of African tradition and her individual integrity. The challenge facing women like Akyebi is to maintain that independence in a way that is compatible with the best of the rural traditions from which they are moving as literate, Westernized, middle-class women.

Akyebi does not reject marriage and motherhood or other crucial institutions of her mother's traditional world. Indeed, notwithstanding her freewheeling declarations of urban independence, she is aided in her running battles with men by the conservative morality that she has inherited from her mother. Above everything else, she is passionately committed to a new and difficult independence as a woman in a world she knows to be frankly male-oriented. This is the kind of explicit knowledge, about the shortcomings as well as strengths of women, that informs the works of these minor writers as well as the major writers.

They all insist that the experience and roles of women are distinguishable from men's, and not usually on equitable grounds. In these works, the woman's experience revolves around her self-perception rather than around the man's needs. The major figures among these writers are the ones who are able to communicate this kind of female self-perception in complex and intense terms—in works that are often artistically imaginative and innovative. These writers are the main focus of the rest of this study—Buchi Emecheta, Efua Sutherland, Ama Ata Aidoo, Flora Nwapa, and Bessie Head. Generally, the protest of all these writers is directed at sexual inequality in traditional as well as modern Africa. This protest is usually interwoven with a frank emphasis on the woman's own need to develop and assert her own strength of will. It is not enough to complain about one's sexual victimization: one needs to do something about it. Buchi Emecheta started out primarily as a protest writer whose early scathing indictment of male chauvinism in England and Nigeria is passionate and direct, but often marred by sloppiness and a long-winded preachiness that leaves little room for complex and credible characterization. As she has matured her fiction has become more complex, blending the continuing notes of protest with interesting, often arresting characterization and with a more interesting narrative style.

Aidoo and Sutherland have received most of the limited attention that has so far been paid to African women writers. They succeed very well in integrating their treatment of women with the literary forms in which they work. As dramatists they suggest that the conventions of the theater and the sexual conventions are analogous to each other, in so far as they involve self-conscious patterns of role-playing. The roles of their theater are therefore deliberately modeled on prevailing sexual roles in society. Moreover, as a short-story writer Aidoo develops her techniques in such a way that each story becomes a direct, structural reflection of the personality of the woman it describes.

In a purely quantitative sense, Flora Nwapa's two novels represent a limited output, but on the whole her achievement is considerable. Notwithstanding the literate apparatus and precedents of her chosen medium she has developed her novels into what is almost an oral form. The language and structure of each work duplicate the oral and strongly communal environment of her rural women. In re-creating that environment as concretely as she does, Nwapa effectively dramatizes her characters' private desires, as women, against a communal background which thwarts or inhibits their private selves. Finally, her work as novelist exemplifies that highly effective sense of style and form which accounts for her impressive achievement as a short-story writer.

Bessie Head brings to her novels an intense moral idealism which is effectively counterbalanced by her harshly realistic images of sexism, racism, and economic injustice. But in the Bessie Head novel these external forces of evil and oppression are always intertwined with the private lives and self-awareness of her characters. The question of power is not only an external political issue. It is also a moral and psychological crisis in each individual. The solutions to social problems therefore rest on the individual's personal strength, as well as on institutional reforms. On this basis, Bessie Head is one of the most profoundly representative of the artists discussed here. Her social vision is focused on matters of immediate and concrete African significance. At the same time, she raises questions about the nature of female self-awareness, about the need for female self-help and inner strength, that are fraught with implications for women everywhere. Like the other writers, but more explicitly than most, she is speaking on behalf of and about the African woman, while compelling our attention as a voice for all women.

3   Buchi Emecheta

Of all the women writers in contemporary African literature Buchi Emecheta of Nigeria has been the most sustained and vigorous voice of direct, feminist protest. Only Bessie Head of South Africa, compares with Emecheta in a certain intensity and directness when describing sexual inequality and female dependency. Even Bessie Head moves away from this kind of direct, intense confrontation with a male-oriented world, after her first novel *(When Rain Clouds Gather)* and, as we shall see in due course, her subsequent works have shifted to an increasingly introspective emphasis on the woman's inner self, while the element of protest, though still remaining significant, has receded into the background.

In Emecheta we detect a similar development, an increasing emphasis on the woman's sense of self, as the writer has matured and as that maturity enables her to deal more and more adeptly and convincingly with the subtleties of characterization and private introspectiveness. With Emecheta the fervor and rhetoric of protest —that is, the explicit and unequivocal denunciation of the sexual status quo—have not diminished. If anything, she has become a more effective protest writer precisely because she has been increasingly successful in blending the rhetoric of impassioned protest with her maturing talent for characterization.

After an early school education in Lagos, Emecheta was married at seventeen, and eventually emigrated in 1962 to join her husband who was then a student in England. They eventually separated and she studied for a degree in sociology from the University of London while supporting her five children. In addition to writing she has worked as a sociologist in London.

To date Buchi Emecheta has published four books; *In the Ditch* (1973), *Second Class Citizen* (1974), *The Bride Price* (1976), and *The Slave Girl* (1977).[1] The first two are autobiographies written in a fictional format in which only the names, including the author's, have been changed—this is according to Emecheta's assurance in the foreword to *In the Ditch*. This first book describes Adah Obi's struggle to survive in London's slums, living on public welfare (the dole) with five children after having separated from her husband. The second work actually takes us to the beginning, tracing Adah's fortunes, and misfortunes, from childhood in the Nigerian village of Ibuza. She gets a secondary school education despite the indifference and hostility of her family, obtains a good job as a librarian in Lagos, where she marries before leaving to join her husband in London. Once in London, she discovers that the radical changes in environment and economic situation are too much for their marriage and a separation soon follows a succession of quarrels, beatings, and unplanned pregnancies. With *The Bride Price*, her first full-fledged novel, Emecheta takes a holiday from her own life to describe the tragedy of a young Nigerian woman who defies the customs of family and society by rejecting an arranged marriage in order to wed an outcast, the descendant of slaves.

The effectiveness of Emecheta's protest is often undercut by her shortcomings as a writer. All three works suffer from lapses into banal statement and into what is, quite simply, sloppy writing that deserves more careful editing than it apparently received. Adah's description of a friend is a good example of this problem: "Adah was sorry for her, particularly as, although she was very beautiful in a film-star type of way with smooth, glossy skin, a perfect figure and thick beautiful hair, she was at least thirty" (*Second Class Citizen*, p. 153). Even more self-defeatingly, her criticisms of African men are often marred by generalizations that are too shrill and transparently overstated to be altogether convincing. Thus, when Adah hears that an African student is about to abandon his pregnant English girlfriend she "cursed all African men for treating women the way they do" (*In the Ditch*, p. 157). The indictment fails to be convincing, especially in a work devoted to the disadvantages of women in *English* society, precisely because the example of male callousness which Adah chooses to attribute to African men in some special way is so patently shared by non-

African men in this work and throughout Emecheta's writing as a whole. In the circumstances, the generalization seems to be merely spiteful rather than really illuminating.

In addition to these lapses in style and tone, Emecheta's rhetoric of protest often betrays symptoms of an uncritical response to Western modes of perceiving, and describing Africans. Africans appear too often as "natives" in her works, and there are the familiar Western contrasts between "civilization," on the one hand, and Nigerian "superstitions" or crudeness, on the other. This acceptance of the old Eurocentric standards is all the more disconcerting, and self-defeating, in a writer who is so obviously preoccupied with inequality and oppression as they are manifest in both language and social custom. Note, by way of contrast, how carefully she integrates the nuances of everyday language with pervasive habits of female submissiveness:

[The nurse] looked at Adah for a long time, and then smiled. "Is Victor your only child?"
Adah shook her head, Vicky was not, there was another, but she was only a girl.
"Only a girl? What do you mean by 'only a girl'? She is a person, too, you know, just like your son."

Adah knew all that. But how was she to tell this beautiful creature that in her society she could only be sure of the love of her husband and the loyalty of her parents-in-law by having and keeping alive as many children as possible, and that though a girl may be counted as one child, to her people a boy was like four children put together? (*Second Class Citizen*, p. 62).

There is also some ambiguity in Emecheta's perception of women in Africa and Europe. The scorn of Ibo men and their treatment of women is consistent enough: Ibo men like Francis (Adah's husband) see their wives as sexual conveniences, domestic help, and breeders (preferably of sons) to be beaten, if need be, into submission (*Second Class Citizen*, pp. 164-65). Especially in *In the Ditch*, poor women of all races and national backgrounds share the humiliations and hardships that flow from the double handicap of being poor and female in London. But however much she decries the disadvantages of Nigerian women and of the women in Britain's slums, Adah tends to be naive in her assumptions about the "liberated" comforts of the middle-class Englishwoman. Before the collapse of her marriage, Adah's real goal in London is "just to be a housewife" in the mold of the women's magazines she has been reading in England: "that was all she asked of life. Just to be a mother and a wife" (*Second Class Citizen*, p. 163). In both of the works that are set in London (that is, the first two titles) there is no indication that Emecheta recognizes any significant parallels between the imposed limitations of being born "only" as a girl and the "liberation" that is based on "just" being a housewife. At this point, in spite of Emecheta's repeated invectives against sexual inequality, her reader is left with the impression that sexual equality, as such, tends to be secondary in her work to another issue: the aspiration of poor women, in both urban England and rural Nigeria, towards the relative (material) comforts and security of the married middle-class woman in Western culture—even if the acquisition of those comforts involve a certain degree of dependence on the male. Adah's Francis is therefore reprehensible when he treats his wife as mere convenience for his sexual and domestic needs in the impoverished circumstances of an unsuccessful African student in London; but in Adah's *middle-class dreams* the man's woman is no longer a mere sexual convenience but a wife, not simply a breeder but a mother, and to be "just" a housewife is not a demeaning restriction but a carefully defined and deliberately limited choice of roles—roles, however, which do not seem intrinsically different from the one she fulfils in real, *lower-class*, life.

It is important to note this basic ambiguity in Emecheta's assumption about the needs of her women because it suggests that she does not readily fit into the ranks of those middle-class feminists in the West who are now discovering her works.[2] The fierce denunciation of sexual inequality brings her more closely to the militant temper and rhetoric of contemporary feminism in Europe and the United States than any other female writer in Black Africa, with the possible exception of Bessie Head. As the stronger features of her first work demonstrate, she has used her personal experiences in Europe (as wife, mother, student, and sociologist) to advantage, and in the process has produced the only major body of writing by an African woman about the situation of women in the West. But, however naturally she may appeal to Western feminists because of these aspects of her work, Emecheta also has to be read and understood as an African or Third World writer whose quest for improvements in the situation of women is shaped by considerations that are of more immediate consequence to the non-Western, non-middle-class woman. Much of the feminist movement in the West appeals to women who elect to forego the comfortable dependency of being "just" housewife and mother.[3] For Third World women like the Nigerian Adah Obi (that is, Buchi Emecheta herself) there is a different order of priorities. Having been born into relative poverty and in a society which limits opportunities to rise to middle-class income and status, Emecheta's Adah is more interested in achieving these comforts than she is with raising questions about the lives of middle-class women who have already been "liberated" from dirty tenements and economically inadequate husbands.

In the final analysis, entrenched notions of male privilege and female inferiority are galling to Emecheta, not so much as questions of moral principle but as barriers to survival and self-improvement among poor women in England and emerging or developing countries like Nigeria. Her ambiguity on the subject of sexual injustice, reflects a certain ideological fuzziness, or a certain degree of naiveté, about middle-class status as a key to the unquestionable fulfilment of women as individuals and free persons. However, that very ambiguity flows from one of her significant achievements in describing the lives of British and Nigerian women: by linking the disadvantages of women with the handicaps of poverty, Emecheta places the experiences of her women within a broad context of social injustices in Great Britain, the West as a whole, and the Third World. Curiously enough, Emecheta has tried to minimize the degree to which her work links the woman's experience with other social and economic issues. In her foreword to *In the Ditch*, for example, she writes that the experiences described in the work "were not . . . much affected by the fact that I came from another country and am black" (p. ix). *In the Ditch* hardly supports its author's disclaimer. It is true that Adah Obi's poverty and her difficulties as a single parent in the slums of London are shared by "many women, white and black, living in an over-industrialised society" (p. ix), but it is difficult to ignore the frequent references to race in the work, for Adah is always being reminded by friends and foes, whites and blacks, that she is black, with *her* own people. There is no mistaking the care with which the author develops parallels and analogies between Adah's condition as an impoverished woman and her identity as a black African. Adah sees the dead end of her life in the slums as a symptom of the triple hardship of being orphaned, black, and female: "It is a curse to be an orphan, a double curse to be a black one in a white country, an unforgivable calamity to be a woman with five kids but without a husband" (p. 81).

Pussy Cat Mansions, the public-housing tenements she shares with other poor London families, has actually developed its own hierarchy: relatively well-to-do families like the Smalls lord it over the poorer families with men as bread-winners, and in turn everyone feels superior to fatherless families on the dole. Moreover, this local pecking order is really a grotesque imitation of the oppressive hierarchies in the society at large; and in the racial scheme of things the white Mr. Small quickly puts Adah in her place as a black African (p. 21). In effect, Pussy Cat Mansions is the microcosm of a caste system based on race, sex, class, and property. The entrenched attitudes which expect the worst of Africans and West Indians simply because they are black are analogous to the prevailing, institutionalized attitudes towards the "mums" (the unsupported or single mothers) of Pussy Cat Mansions and other public-housing projects. The "mums" are neglected by the government agencies that are in charge of their welfare, and at best their needs are met with barely disguised contempt or indifference. They are society's ditch-dwellers, relegated to the bottom of their society by virtue of their poverty and their status as women without men, and acting out those irresponsible and self-defeating inclinations (alcohol, overeating, and overbreeding) which society expects of them, partly because such actions offer them an emotional outlet of sorts and partly because they are a means of wreaking a limited vengeance on the caste system itself. For someone like Adah these tactics, and the situation out of which they arise, are quite similar to the familiar patterns of black survival: "One of the methods she had found very helpful in securing friendship in England was to pretend to be stupid. You see, if you were black and stupid, you were conforming to what society expected of you" (pp. 22-23).

This caste system rests on what Emecheta's Adah describes as "industrial culture." The term is never fully developed in the work, largely because of Emecheta's tendency to use vague phrases, or sweeping generalizations, as substitute for precise definitions. Her treatment of industrial culture seems to focus primarily on a tradition, in highly technological societies, of generating systems. Systematization as a prerequisite for technological efficiency seems to have become a self-serving function in Adah's London. Systems of all kinds (government bureaucracies, business organizations, and charity groups) have become closed, self-justifying entities incapable of responding to the human needs that they were conceived of to serve. The caste system of race, sex, and property is therefore an integral part of a cultural environment, industrial culture, which brutalizes the individual and which finds its most vulnerable victims in women who are poor, without jobs or husbands, and with several children. Consequently, while Adah takes pains to denounce the sexual hierarchy of her own Ibo culture, England's sexual caste system is particularly oppressive to her because the very industrial economy which promises so many options and so much freedom to the Nigerian woman in London has effectively combined the caste systems of sex, race, and property with the systems of government and business into a gigantic and faceless "system" (to use Adah's favorite word) that is really antihuman.

The system is also antilife. Its quintessential symbol, Pussy Cat Mansions, is appropriately built on an old cemetery. Despite the sexual (life-force) connotations of its name, the tenement building represents the denial of sex and sexual relationships as fulfilling experience. The mum must often give up her husband because the curious logic of the welfare system makes it easier to live on public assistance if she lives without the father of her children. Having placed her on the dole, the system makes it difficult for her to develop sexual relationships since her dole would be cut off on the assumption that the new man is a breadwinner. In these circumstances sex, when it is available to the mums, is loveless and furtive, a short-term palliative or another way of getting back at the system, and it perpetuates the vicious cycle by leading to more unplanned and unwanted children (pp. 69-70). Adah never really develops an effective way of dealing successfully with the system. She and the other mums do share a certain camaraderie which enables them to ignore or cope with much of the bleakness of their lives, but this kind of friendship has a limited usefulness. It is an association of helpless people whose intimacy is based on the fact that they have accepted the hopelessness of their situation; this remains true despite Adah's wistful tendency to see the spontaneous and natural friendships of the ditch-dwellers as a humane alternative to the regulated, intellectual, artificial style of the system (p. 106).

They exploit their camaraderie in a successful protest that leads to their relocation to better accommodations and to the eventual demolition of the dreadful "Pussy." In the final analysis, their ability to survive in spite of society depends on the willingness of each woman to recover the initiative in her own life and to recapture the personal strength which society and its systems had undermined in the first place. Emecheta realistically places Adah and the other mums face-to-face with one of the hard facts in the lives of all disadvantaged groups trying to climb out of the ditch: however easily the blame for their condition can be attributed to the failings of an external system, their individual recovery and personal integrity can only be assured from within themselves. One of the strengths of *In the Ditch* lies in Emecheta's refusal to offer nicely contrived visions of a totally reorganized and harmonized social order. The system remains as indifferently powerful as ever, and although the women's revolt as a group has led to some improvement in their surroundings it has not really lessened the ingrained insensitivity of the bureaucracy, or their dependence on the system as a whole. In fact, women like Adah's best friend, Whoopey, are even deeper in the ditch at the conclusion, living in a new apartment, but (in Whoopey's case) with a new baby on the way and the same lack of prospects or initiative.

Adah's own dependence is underscored by her procrastination when it is her turn to vacate Pussy Cat Mansions. Horrible as the place is, it is familiar; the demoralized Adah finds it much easier to cling to the familiar decay of the Mansions and their solacing friendships, than to start afresh elsewhere. When she does move it is with the recognition that she must accept full responsibility for her own survival and selfhood. That recognition is a crucial first step for Adah and other women like herself whose age-old sexual roles (both in Nigeria and England) have combined with the patronizing bureauracies of industrial culture to create the most crucial ditch of all, the psychological ditch of female dependency. There are no guarantees that Adah will eventually escape from that ditch, and this absence of guarantees is heightened by the enduring strength of the social systems around her. Emecheta has made her point in Adah's last-minute recognition of her own responsibilities to herself. Notwithstanding the need to denounce the destructiveness of external systems, and without minimizing the value of sisterhood among the mums of her world, the ultimate solution rests with the individual woman alone, for she must recapture the initiative and restore the inner strength that has been sapped by poverty and institutionalized dependency.

This kind of argument seems to pose a difficult paradox for Emecheta's women. Having lost her initiative, or having lacked an independent spirit in the first place, how does a woman set about acquiring any degree of self-sufficiency? Emecheta's contention is that even in the most unpromising circumstances the individual never really loses the potential for choice and strength, and it is crucial to note that Adah manages to continue her education (despite formidable obstacles) because she is determined to escape the slum and its humiliations. Thus, it remains the individual's ultimate responsibility, even in the most unlikely circumstances, to develop what is essentially an indestructible strength of will—as Emecheta perceives it.

This thematic argument provides a clue, even in this first uneven work, to Emecheta's real forte as a protest writer. There is protest in the familiar sense of complaint and recrimination, but it is already being integrated with the emphasis on a certain kind of critical introspectiveness. Instead of simple denunciation, in the manner of most run-of-the-mill protest writers, she is already beginning to deal simultaneously with both the deficiencies in the woman's environment and the shortcomings in the woman's self-awareness. The result is a relatively complex vision helping to offset the thinness of style and occasional fuzziness, and focusing increasingly in her later work on growth or capacity for growth in the individual woman.

This emphasis on individual growth and self-reliance is more fully developed in *Second Class Citizen*, which is actually set in the period prior to the first work. This work depicts the gradual erosion of Adah's confidence and independence in London, following a fairly successful career in Nigeria. The young girl Adah is an irrepressible spirit who successfully defies the conventions of family and social custom to gain an education and begin an independent life as a young librarian in Lagos. Although her successes come at the expense of her relationship with a conservative family, Adah actually credits that conservative background with having encouraged the development of her independent spirit. Since children, especially girls, are taught to be useful in her society, "Adah learned very early to be responsible for herself. Nobody was interested in her for her own sake, only in the money she would fetch, and the housework she could do and Adah, happy at being given the opportunity of survival, did not waste time thinking about its rights or wrongs. She had to survive" (p. 18). Her marriage to Francis Obi, a young clerk in Lagos, helps to ensure the realization of her childhood dreams—a fairly comfortable middle-class life style, complete with four maids, a well-paying job at the American Consulate library, and the daily gratification of coming home to "be waited on hand and foot, and in the evening be made love to" (p. 26). Eventually Francis leaves to study for an accounting degree in London. Adah follows him with their children, only to discover that unemployment and failure as a student have changed her husband for the worse. At first she tries to hold the family together as its breadwinner, but her growing family compounds their problems since Francis' cultural background, with its emphasis on childbearing, does not allow him to support birth control. Their lives slide into the inevitable dissolution of the marriage and the work ends with Adah starting life in London on her own with five small children.

It is easy enough to isolate the villains in the growing list of Adah's misfortunes, from the family members who begrudge young women an education to the embittered husband who bullies and beats her, but the protagonist is not always as admirable as the work seems to imply. Despite her pious complaints about the evils of female subordination and the exploitiveness of men in Ibo society, she is not above being manipulative in her turn. She marries Francis, not out of love, but simply because a teenaged girl living alone in Lagos (as a librarian) "would be asking for trouble" (p. 23). The casualness with which she enters and describes her loveless marriage is the more striking when we remember her own invectives against parents who sell their daughters into loveless matches for the profit of the bride price, and, even more disconcertingly, neither Adah nor Emecheta seems aware of or concerned about the apparent inconsistency. Moreover, although Adah grows to loathe Francis' sexual demands in London, she is quite capable on occasion of manipulating his sexual desires in order to exact a promise or commitment from him before giving in to him (pp. 85-86). In fact Adah is less than honest throughout the work about her own sexuality or her sexual relationship with Francis. He is repeatedly crucified as the typical example of the male's absurd and humiliating sexuality. Francis strutting around the flat while he lectures her on the alleged virtues of female submissiveness is a sexual caricature, at once grotesque and menacing: "his sex was inside [his] baggy trousers, dangling this way and that like the pendulum of Big Ben. . . . It dangled much more furiously now, this way, that way, and back again, because he was excited" (p. 100). Adah's contempt for Francis' sexuality quickly broadens into derision for what she sees as the animal image of everyone "when we are consumed by our basic desires" (p. 86).

That touch of hauteur is not convincing, neither is the shrill and repeated repugnance for Francis' animality, for the truth seems to be that her condemnation is less motivated by a consistent moral judgement than it is by a need to absolve herself of any responsibility for the love-making that leads to her frequent pregnancies. Note, for example, how easily her account of her first night in London (after months of separation) passes rapidly, in turn, from an admission of shared passion and mutual longing, to an uneasiness about possible pregnancy, to an attack on Francis' irrationality and selfishness: "They made up for it that night, forgetting, in their intense disappointment and loneliness. . . . that they were not supposed to have more children for some time. . . . But how could she protest to a man who was past reasoning? The whole process was an attack, as savage as that of any animal" (p. 40). Emecheta has obviously been at pains to present Francis' indifference to birth control as an example of male callousness sanctioned by Ibo culture, yet she remains curiously unaware of her alter ego's lack of candor about her own sexual response to her husband.

Adah scorns Ibos and their materialism, both at home and abroad, but she sounds rather hollow in view of her own pride in achieving middle-class status and security in Lagos. If she is aware of the contradiction between her professed scorn of the "Ibo elite" and her own single-minded ambition to join the middle-class elite of Lagos she shows her readers no sign of this—despite the description of her Lagos phase as "escape into elitism." Again, Emecheta seems disturbingly unaware of the inconsistencies in her alter ego's behavior and judgements.

Indeed, neither Emecheta nor Adah seems concerned with the relationship, or lack of relationship, between Adah's social judgements (on sexism, middle-class Philistinism, or the African aping of Western customs) and Adah's own career. The author's protest, as political statement, represents a grasp of the links and analogies between social and political issues, and this appears as early as *In the Ditch*. But her protest tends to be narrowly political, or partisan, in the making of judgements, and it fails to convince that its moral motives are any more consistent or real than those of the author's targets. In spite of the tone and rhetoric of moral indignation, there remains a curious amorality about both *Second Class Citizen* and its predecessor. The "Ibo elite" is reprehensible, not because its conduct raises basic questions about the role or very existence of elites, but because its age-old traditions of male privilege pose barriers to the ambitious Adahs of the society. What is of central importance is Adah's ambition to be successful and independent by way of all those middle-class achievements which are being opened up to the males of the new African states but which have been all but closed, Adah feels, to women.

Adah's criteria are achievement and ambition, dramatized by her childhood dreams of education and by her early success in Lagos, and further underscored by her eventual failures in London. Throughout all of this we are always aware of that fundamental thesis which Emecheta develops without equivocation and inconsistencies: failure or success is ultimately determined not by external obstacles as such, be they African sexism or English poverty, but by the individual's strength of will and independence of spirit. Adah the strong-willed child grows up into the determined and relatively successful young librarian in Lagos because her independent spirit refuses to accept predefined roles of female subordination. Conversely, this independence has always inspired a certain contempt for conventionally submissive women whose limited personalities "had a way of sapping" Adah's own self-confidence (p. 12).

On the other hand, Adah the London housewife is a failure throughout much of the second half of the work because she has all but lost her self-confidence under the shock of a new country, a changed husband, and all the unaccustomed humiliations of poverty, filthy housing, and unplanned pregnancies. She had set out, in that ship to London, to achieve first-class status because "It's nice to be treated like an elite, a status they were achieving" (p. 34). In London she finds that she is a second-class citizen, as her husband warns her on her first night: "In Lagos . . . you may be earning a million pounds a day; you may have hundreds of servants; you may be living like an elite, but the day you land in England, you are a second-class citizen. So you can't discriminate against your own people, because we are all second-class" (p. 39). Adah has discovered that the situation against which she has rebelled all of her life, the woman's second-class status vis-à-vis the man, has become the dominant reality of her life in London: to her husband "a woman was a second-class human, to be slept with at any time, even during the day, and, if she refused, to have sense beaten into her until she gave in" (pp. 164-65). She has also discovered that the woman as second-class human is also the central symbol of her world: the poor (especially the Irish and poor immigrant students) are second-class citizens's in England's socioeconomic system, Africans are second-class in Europe, blacks are second-class in a white society, and emerging Third World countries still retain second-class status in spite of intellectual and economic borrowings from the first-class West.

As for Adah herself, she is in danger of becoming a second-class citizen in the most crucial sense of the term—in the sense of personal direction and independent self-awareness. She almost lacks the initiative to break out of a marriage which is destroying her emotional and physical resources, and only does so after her husband nearly beats her to death. Her determined pursuit of a university degree, her fierce commitment to a better life for herself and her children, and even that belated decision to leave the marriage all evince the survival of that strong-willed independence that has always motivated her. The ability to survive and to sustain her will is an essentially creative talent, one that is analogous to the creative resources of the artist. Therefore, it is appropriate that during the worst period of poverty and a crumbling marriage, Adah finds time from the demands of job and children to write a novel. A jealous Francis ridicules her attempts to become a writer, because women—especially *African* women—are supposed to be incapable of such a thing (p. 167), and he eventually destroys her manuscript. Her attempt, however, is an important symptom. In keeping with Emecheta's penchant for establishing pointed analogies, the second-class status of being African, female, and poor is counterbalanced by a second set of analogies which constitute a "first-class" capacity for independence and creativity—Adah's pride and ambitions as a student, her protective strength as a mother, and now a newly discovered talent that seems to be another version of motherhood. As a writer she looks upon her novel as a "brain-child," and the act of writing seems to be a form of conception and a kind of birth. In fact Adah's writing has become more than an analogy, it is an act of self-affirmation, proclaiming that inner resourcefulness that refuses to accept the status of second-class citizen. The real strength of *Second Class Citizen* lies in the unusual consistency with which Emecheta develops this theme.

Not surprisingly, the title of Adah's abortive novel is also the title of Emecheta's third book, and her first bona fide novel, *The Bride Price*. There is no indication that the actual novel duplicates its fictional counterpart. In fact, Adah describes her own work as a comedy but the actual novel by Emecheta is decidedly tragic. After her father's death in Lagos the young girl Aku-nna returns to live in his Ibo village, Ibuza, where Aku-nna's uncle "inherits" her mother from his late brother. Aku-nna is allowed to continue her schooling largely because this will enhance her bride price for the benefit of her avaricious uncle. She falls in love with her teacher Chike Ofulue but their marriage is forbidden by ancient taboo since his family is descended from slaves. After Aku-nna is kidnapped by the son of a leading Ibuza family, her own family is obliged, according to ancient custom, to agree to her marriage to her abductor. Chike dramatically rescues Aku-nna from her abductor before the marriage is formalized and they elope to another village where they both find jobs and a comfortable home. Their union not only defies the taboo against intermarriages of "free" and "slave" families, but it also challenges an ancient curse—that any woman who marries against the wishes of her family and whose bride price remains unpaid will die in childbirth. Aku-nna's uncle spitefully refuses to accept the match or the proferred bride price and Aku-nna fulfills the ancient curse when she dies in childbirth.

Aku-nna's fate and the effectiveness of the curse are not altogether what they seem on the surface, particularly in view of Emecheta's frank and repeated contempt for all religions, for "native superstitions" and Roman Catholic "rigamarole" alike. Aku-nna does not die because of the mysterious intervention of the supernatural—notwithstanding her uncle's malevolent incantations and those omnipotent powers that she is supposed to have defied by her marriage. She literally dies of the fear that the curse will be effective, and on this basis her death flows from the novel's central thesis: that fate or destiny in its most significant sense is not based on the mysterious predispositions of inscrutable supernatural forces, but on the function of social institutions and the shaping patterns of cultural traditions. In the woman's experience, fate is therefore the collective will of the community and the roles that are prescribed by the community. In a subjective, and much more crucial sense, the fate of each woman is ultimately determined by the extent to which she accepts or rejects that collective will.

The story of *The Bride Price* is a study of the relationship between the collective traditions of the communal will and Aku-nna's own strength of will (and in this regard she is the fictional counterpart of the autobiographical Adah Obi). This is the central theme on which Emecheta focuses her novel. The result is a tightly organized structure which is a decided improvement over the episodic fitfulness of *In the Ditch* and which fulfills the promise of *Second Class Citizen* where the development, decline, and last-minute salvaging of Adah's individuality provides the narrative with a definite coherence and an element of suspense. In *The Bride Price* the concern with narrative suspense and development occasionally lends itself to the rather melodramatic scenes of Aku-nna's abduction and subsequent elopement. But on the whole, it works to Emecheta's advantage, delineating Aku-nna's growth from an inexperienced and naive childhood into a knowing and rebellious womanhood. The narrative development is heightened by the pervasive sense of a malevolent and increasingly menacing destiny, from the sudden death of Aku-nna's father to her own deathbed terror of an avenging deity. Emecheta's central theme also benefits from the manner in which the tightly controlled narrative flows for the most part through Aku-nna's consciousness and at regular but limited intervals through external viewpoints (of mother, uncle, cousins, and future husband) which focus directly on Aku-nna herself (as daughter, bride-price bait, age-group member, and wife respectively). Within this subjective context Emecheta's narrative presents both the communal will and Aku-nna's personality simultaneously by emphasizing the manner in which Aku-nna grows up into womanhood. Her growth is, simultaneously, the development of her own personality and will, and her perception of the rituals, the values, and the institutions through which her community celebrates its traditions and exercises its will. In turn, these rituals and their attendant sense of proper form permeate Emecheta's narrative form with a definite sense of proportion. Her fictive structure is beginning to become a direct symptom of her thematic concerns.

Consequently the various forms or modes of Aku-nna's culture are carefully defined, as she becomes aware of them, through a series of dramatic episodes all of which are centered on the fundamental issues of life, death, puberty, marriage, and childbirth. All of these episodes are presented by way of appropriate rituals (the burial ceremony, the wake-songs and dances for her dead father, the prescribed fertility rites which Aku-nna's mother undergoes in hopes of having a second son, the sanctioned practice of abducting a woman in order to force her family's agreement to a marriage with her abductor, and the fertility dances which Aku-nna's age-group rehearses to celebrate the transition to womanhood). At the very least, these episodes are associated with a sense of propriety, with an emphasis on whatever has been traditionally defined to be *correct*. Note the natural, even inevitable, manner in which Aku-nna's relatives assume responsibilities for the mourning and the children's welfare after the father's death, or the carefully correct manner in which Chike Olufue's father attempts to break through his age-old status as "oshu," the descendant of slaves, in order to persuade Aku-nna's family to accept and sanction her marriage.

Aku-nna gradually learns about her culture's institutions and values, on two levels, First, the appropriate rituals initiate her into the significance of life and death for the individual and for the community's particular traditions. Like her young brother she has no real awareness of death until her father dies, and their involvement in the ceremonies of burial and mourning shock her into the acceptance of death as an inescapable part of life itself. In a similar vein, the fertility dances for which her age group prepares coincide with the arrival of her own menstrual cycle to impress upon her those physical and emotional patterns of individual growth which are integrated with universal cycles of life, death, and birth.

Second, Aku-nna's rapid maturity is measured by her growing awareness of those points at which her culture's traditions determine the fate of women in her society. Thus, the ceremonies of burial and mourning not only mark her father's death as such, but they are also a prelude to the established custom of transferring the widow and her children to the surviving brother who elects to exercise his right of inheritance—a practice which emerges in the novel as one of several symptoms of the woman's status as possession rather than person. The arrival of her menstrual cycle not only signalizes Aku-nna's physical maturity into womanhood, it also coincides with the growing rebelliousness with which she views the significance of a woman's physical maturity in her culture. She is now ripe for marriage to anyone upon whom her uncle decides for his mercenary advantage. Her mother's frantic attempts to have a-nother son impress upon the young woman the degree to which the full humanity of women is defined on the basis of a highly specialized usefulness—the ability to bear sons. As she recognizes the extent to which institutions and traditions limit the woman's per-

sonality, Aku-nna is increasingly aware of the manner in which
these limits are comparable with other forms of restricted individuality in her culture.

In keeping with Emecheta's pattern of protest by analogy, the
novel invites parallels between the situation of the Ibo women and
the traditional patterns of discrimination against those individuals
whose ancestors served as slaves in (precolonial) Ibo households.
Consequently, when Aku-nna marries Chike, the descendant of
slaves, Emecheta's narrative analogy between women and slaves is
underscored by the sexual union: both groups are denied full equality with the males of "free" families and both are subjected to
restrictive taboos (the elaborate description of taboos on women
during their menstrual periods proceeds simultaneously with the
suspenseful unfolding of Chike's secret, and taboo, courtship). In
effect, Aku-nna's marriage is not only the symbolic celebration of
her physical growth (she elopes with Chike shortly after her own
menstrual cycle begins). It is also symbolic in another sense, for it
is the ceremonial climax of her rebellion against entrenched sexual
roles and other social customs which she perceives as limiting and
demeaning.

Here, too, Emecheta reveals that realistic insight which is one of
the saving graces of *In the Ditch*. Aku-nna's rebellion is real enough,
but the traditions against which she rebels persist to the end of the
novel, in much the same way that the system perseveres in the
earlier work. If both the name and actual birth of her daughter Joy
celebrate the vitality and creative self-consciousness that are inherent in Aku-nna's rebellion, then Aku-nna's death marks the
extent to which that rebellion is incomplete. The traditions against
which she rebels are too strongly entrenched in her society and
their attendant sanctions are still too dominant in her own mind,
and she cannot be completely emancipated from and immune to
them. Her death is itself a demonstration of the degree to which her
will is still dominated despite her conscious acts of revolt.

The nature of Aku-nna's development and the implications of
her death reflect the novelist's frankness about the ambiguities and
contradictions, even the backslidings, of her rebel-protagonist.
This is the kind of frankness that is sometimes lacking in the two
autobiographical works in which the scoring of political points

lends itself too easily to partisan single-mindedness and to thin moral judgements. In *The Bride Price*, there is a more candid, and therefore more interesting, preoccupation with those unresolved internal conflicts which are inseparable from the equally unresolved tensions between the rebellious woman and the status quo. On balance, Emecheta who has devoted so much of her writing to the growth of her women, is now beginning to show signs of her own maturity as a novelist.

These signs of maturity continue to be evident in her fourth work. *The Slave Girl* (1977) is close, in some respects, to the mood and themes of *The Bride Price*. In this last novel there is a brooding sense of fate—the same sense of a socially and historically defined destiny that molds the woman's identity and role in *The Bride Price*. In *The Slave Girl*, too, this destiny is linked with that tradition-rooted sense of order which shapes the history and values of the woman's community. And of even more immediate significance, the slave motif of the preceding novel is more fully developed. The institution of slavery, local African slavery, is again a cultural symptom of what Emecheta deplores as the woman's servile status in African societies. As in *The Bride Price*, the symbolism of slavery is even more crucial when it is applied to the woman's private sense of self. Her dependency, apathy, and ingrained habit of accepting a subordinate status—all these habits are e-quated, even more explicitly than in the preceding work, with a slave mentality that lacks the strength of will and innate resiliency which Emecheta has consistently opposed to oppressive systems and traditions of all kinds.

As in *The Bride Price*, the narrative plot of *The Slave Girl* centers on the life of a young Ibo woman in rural Nigeria, and the story begins with her childhood. Here, however, it is the woman herself who is an actual slave. Ojebeta is born early in the twentieth century in the village of Ibuza, the first child to survive to her parents after a long series of still births and infant deaths. When she is still a small child both parents succumb to influenza, a strange new disease that the white colonizers have brought to rural communities like Ibuza. Shortly after her parents' death, Ojebeta is taken by her younger brother to Ontisha, the huge trading center of Eastern Nigeria, and there he sells her to Ma Palagada, a distant relative.

Ma Palagada is one of the more successful "market women," or traders, in Onitsha, and Ojebeta joins her household as one of several slave girls who assist her in the market as well as at home. As Ojebeta grows up to become an attractive young woman, she learns not only what it is like to be a slave but also the limitations of being a woman in her society. As a slave girl she sees and experiences the slave's absolute lack of rights and privileges. When she eventually obtains her freedom (following Ma Palagada's death) she discovers that being a "free" woman does not liberate her from the male prerogatives of her world. As a woman she is still a possession, a man's possession. Although the man in this case is her husband, whom she marries shortly after leaving the Palagadas, the novel emphasizes that Objebeta has simply exchanged one kind of servitude for another. This is the rather grimly ironic note on which the novel ends.

Apart from these thematic similarities with *The Bride Price*, this fourth work is conceived on a more ambitious scale than Emecheta's earlier works. The woman's relationship with her community is set against a broad historical background, one which links Ojebeta's personal story with the history of her village, with contemporary events in colonial Africa as a whole, and, finally, with a universal panorama of the unending cycles of life and death. The prologue to the novel therefore describes the founding of Ojebeta's village, generations before her birth, by an Ibo prince. He had settled in this section of Nigeria after having been exiled from his own community due to the accidental death of his opponent in a wrestling match. In effect, Ibuza was created out of death itself.

This introductory emphasis on the creation of life out of death serves as a preface to the birth of Ojebeta herself. Since she is the first child to survive after so many deaths she is literally an example of life emerging from death, and in this regard the birth is a microcosm of Ibuza's own history. At the same time, the history of the village and the circumstances of Ojebeta's birth are analogous to the broader sweep of contemporary African history. The destructive presence of the Europeans, from the early slave traders to the colonial rulers, involves a death of sorts, one that is symbolized by the havoc which is wreaked on the African population by the

European disease. This is the death of old African traditions. The people in Ojebeta's village have the disturbing impression that since the arrival of the Europeans their own world has changed for the worse: the "felenza" (influenza) had carried away the men who were men, and now the survivors had been left only with the "ghosts of men" (p. 79). One of these "ghosts" is Okolie, the brother who sells Ojebeta into slavery. He is a ne'er-do-well who eventually sneaks away from the village to look for a white man's job after he has failed miserably as a farmer and as a husband (pp. 84-85).

In turn, this cultural death implies the birth of a new, rather unsettling, and chaotic order. This recurrent emphasis on deaths of all kinds establishes the continuous nature of the life-death cycle itself. Within a few short years after her own birth and survival affirm the continuity of life, Ojebeta learns about another continuity —that of death—when the influenza epidemic wipes out her parents and several other villagers. At that time it seems to her "that the whole world was dying, one by one" (p. 27).

Although the scale on which she operates is somewhat broader here, Emecheta continues to underscore the links between women and their community as the central issue of her fiction. The historical references and the sense of continuity that they evoke reinforce the familiar impression of a malignant human destiny that influences the woman's experience. This influence is emphasized quite early in the novel, as early as the occasion of Ojebeta's birth. The woman who acts as midwife cannot enter the compound of Ojebeta's father because it is taboo for a woman to be in the house of a titled man when she is menstruating—that is, when she is "unclean." The passing reference to the taboo is almost casual, but its implications are central to the narrative themes. Emecheta is clearly drawing our attention to the degree to which the woman's body is her fate, in a limiting and invidious sense, for it is really a kind of biological destiny designed by society rather than by nature, one that limits her identity, surrounds her with taboos, and even restricts her physical mobility. As in *The Bride Price*, this kind of limitation is akin to slavery.

Emecheta handles the theme of slavery on the broad kind of scale on which she develops the issues of history, life, and death in the novel. Thus, Ojebeta's experience as a slave girl is related to (1) indigenous slavery in Africa itself, (2) the history of the European slave trade in Africa, and African complicity in that trade, and (3) slavery as an allegory of the woman's traditional status in society, irrespective of whether she is technically "slave" or "free." Emecheta is unsparing in her handling of African slave traders and slave owners, making no distinctions between the local practice and the European version. In this regard she is comparable with Ama Ata Aidoo of Ghana whose play, *Anowa*, declines to engage in the curious distinctions which some historians have offered between one kind of slavery (the "benign" African tradition) and the other ("brutal") European practice.

Both writers understandably insist that a slave is a slave is a slave —a mere possession that has been denied his or her humanity. Aidoo, like Emecheta, links the history of African slavery with the tradition of female subordination in her play. In her novel, Emecheta is at deliberate pains to underscore the basic similarities between all forms of slavery, and she draws certain links between African slave traders or slave owners, and their European counterparts. Hours after Okolie sells his young sister into slavery, his attitude and bearing remind the narrator of those days when "it was easy for the European to urge the chief of a powerful village to wage war on a weaker one in order to obtain slaves for the New World" (p. 73). Although Ma Palagada has no direct connections with the old European (trans-Atlantic) slave trade, nonetheless the novelist carefully links the formidable market woman (and slave owner) with the European tradition of colonialism and slavery: as a young woman Palagada was the concubine of a Portuguese man, living, that is, with a representative of the nation that pioneered European slave trading on the West African coast centuries before.

Emecheta has defined slavery as a brutal continuity in human history, one that is interwoven, in this novel, with the historical persistence of women's subordination and powerlessness. Emecheta develops this link rather effectively by dwelling on the emotional and moral implications of slavery itself, for the slave, before examining the psyches of "free" and enslaved women. In emotional and psychological terms slavery impresses upon each slave her essential worthlessness as a human being. Chiago, one of the older slaves in Ma Palagada's household, still remembers a slave girl, in another town, who was buried alive with her master's dead wife, in order to satisfy a technical requirement for the funeral. In a similar vein, the slave's day-to-day existence requires her to accept the status of being a mere thing, because the institution destroys all sense of individuality (p. 72). As a mere thing, the slave is expected to suppress normal self-expression—hence Ma Palagada's slave girls remind the newly enslaved Ojebeta of "wooden dolls" (p. 87).

Slavery is not simply a status or role in Emecheta's novel. It is also a condition, a way of thinking and acting. In keeping with her usual interest in the attitudes, as well as condition, of society's victims, Emecheta insists in this novel on the degree to which the victim—the slave in this instance—contributes to her own victimization, by allowing herself to accept the role of victim. Quite apart from the actual brutality and degradation in being slaves, the most crucial difficulty in the lives of these young women (and a handful of men) is the degree to which they have developed a slave mentality. This mentality allows them to accept, even support, the status quo. One of the men, for example, would never be disloyal to his master (p. 102). Although she manages to remain less servile than most of the other slaves around her, Ojebeta herself is quite capable of feeling grateful for having been enslaved by Ma Palagada, whenever the latter shows some special kindness to her slave (p. 107).

Christianity occupies a somewhat ambiguous role here. On one hand, it is the familiar palliative for the enslaved and the outcast. It gives the slave girls a sense of belonging, of even being special. Church-going allows them to be seen as elite slaves, and a Christian education gives them the literacy which places them several notches above the mere "illiterate pagans." On the other hand, the alien religion is obviously another of those foreign European influences that have helped to undermine local values. To a large extent this ambiguity springs from Emecheta's rather obvious ambivalence towards Christianity. As we have seen in another context, she is contemptuous of organized religion. But while Christianity has helped to erode some local customs, her contempt for some of those customs—especially slavery in this case—make her less than completely hostile to Christianity in this novel. Consequently, Ojebeta's enduring devoutness as Christian is ambiguous. It is a symptom of the degree to which she continues to be largely docile and long-suffering, even after she gains her freedom, but in the final analysis her Christianity is also inseparable from those things, including her inner strength, which enabled her to endure the trauma of slavery.

The issue of the slave's servility is crucial to an understanding of how Emecheta links this theme of slavery with the general experience of women in Ojebeta's world. Emecheta's familiar broadsides against male shortcomings are overshadowed in this work by vigorous and repeated criticism of women as the main accomplices in their own enslavement. In one sense women are slaves as a matter of status. The slave girl figure is therefore a broad sexual archetype. As possessions without freedom or privilege, the girls are sexual objects to be abused and sexually exploited at will by the men in the household. In this respect, they are symbols of the degree to which "free" women are essentially the possessions of the men in their world, first their fathers and brothers, then their husbands. Ojebeta's aunt, Uteh, can therefore be philosophical about the fact that Okolie had sold his sister into slavery. No woman is ever free, she reminds Ojebeta, therefore it is a "great honour" to be owned by a man. Okolie was not too much in the wrong when his actions are viewed in this light, his only real offence being that he failed to turn over the proceeds of the sale to his older brother—the one who had the "right" to sell Ojebeta in the first place (p. 158). Ojebeta soon comes to the conclusion, after leaving the Palagadas, that no woman is really free (p. 168). Even when she marries a man of her own choice she has to accept the fact that custom has made her his property (p. 176).

In another sense, women are also slaves by virtue of their slave mentality, and because of this they are accomplices to their own enslavement—in much the same way that the indigenous traditions of slavery and slave trading made it relatively easy for Africans of another generation to become accomplices in the trans-Atlantic slave trade. Aunt Uteh, for example, accepts the woman's status as a man's possession—she even proclaims that such a status is an honor. As the narrator wryly observes "In Ibuza women were usually more conservative than men" (p. 150). Someone like Aunt Uteh is merely pathetic in this regard. Emecheta is much more contemptuous of women like Ma Palagada and her daughter Victoria (by her Portuguese lover).

Victoria, in particular, is cruel to the slave girls. She never recognizes them as human beings, and she usually treats them as if she were "a bitch with puppies" (p. 113). Ma Palagada's exploitation of the girls and Victoria's cruelty towards them clearly indicate the complicity of the two women in the general status of women as slaves everywhere. Since the narrative establishes that the slave girl is actually a symbol of the woman's universal condition in her society, it follows readily that Victoria and her mother are not simply guilty of perpetuating a slave girl's slavery. They are also contributing, as women, to the female status quo that is represented by the slave girl. Conversely, it is interesting to note that if the men of Ibuza are less conservative than their women, then the men in Ma Palagada's house seem much more susceptible to humane impulses vis-à-vis the slaves than are the women. Victoria's half-brother Clifford (by Ma Palagada's African husband) is an egocentric monster as a boy, but grows up to be a sensitive young man, at least sensitive enough to recognize his own shortcomings, and (for a while) to seek marriage with Ojebeta despite her status as a slave. Pa Palagada softens enough after his wife's death to allow Ojebeta to buy her freedom—something which Ma Palagada never got around to doing before she died. This is also something that Victoria fiercely, but futilely opposes.

The actual purchase of her freedom is not officially completed until after Ojebeta's marriage, for it is only then that she (or her husband Jacob, rather) can repay the Palagadas her slave price. In repaying the Palagadas, Joseph, Ojebeta's husband, is really paying a kind of bride price. This fact, together with the traditional nature of their marriage, emphasizes the degree to which Ojebeta's status remains unchanged at the end of the novel. She is still a possession —with a new master.

The continuation of her enslavement is also attributed to Ojebeta's own accepting mentality. She "was content and did not want more of life; she was happy in her husband, happy to be submissive, even to accept an occasional beating because that was what she had been brought up to believe a wife should expect" (pp. 173-74). This amounts to a new note in Emecheta's fiction. The earlier works pinpoint a certain resiliency and rebelliousness in her women, without minimizing the internal and external obstacles to the woman's full equality. In *The Slave Girl* there is a shift from the previous delicate balance between an inner rebelliousness and an intransigent social order. The vision has become bleaker, and the women are strikingly and unusually (for Emecheta) lacking in the capacity for even an incipient or underdeveloped rebellion.

Women like Ojebeta are their own worst enemies. As such, their personalities reflect Emecheta's insistence on an unpleasant reality: women may very well be their own worst enemies because, after a continuous history of subordination, they often lack the spirit to rebel—or even the awareness that a rebellion is in order. We have moved from the qualified rebelliousness of the earlier works to a bleak realism. The only changes that now take place in the world are external and superficial rather than deep and meaningful. They are simplistically symbolic rather than substantive: "So as Britain was emerging from war once more victorious, and claiming to have stopped the slavery which she had helped to spread in all her black colonies, Ojebeta, now a woman of thirty-five, was changing masters" (p. 179). Emecheta has obviously matured beyond the impassioned but uneven protest of the earlier works, into a writer with an increasingly tough and uncompromising sense of realism. This heralds a promising future.

4   Efua Sutherland

In a discussion of the theater in Ghana, Efua Sutherland once declared that a truly vital theater should heed the example of oral literature by dealing directly with contemporary experience. Oral literature, she pointed out, "uses . . . experience artistically." By a similar token, a national theater should look at and utilize the repositories of a culture's experience, it should avoid the merely imitative art of "performing plays just because they exist in books already," and it therefore should depend on the willingness of the artist to create forms which can communicate both the contemporary experience and the historical process out of which it grew. In this sense, theater becomes a kind of immediate cultural exploration: "There are all sorts of exciting things to venture and I take a deep breath and venture forth, . . . I'm on a journey of discovery. I'm discovering my own people." Sutherland's views and practice find a ready supporter in Ama Ata Aidoo: "What she conceives," Aidoo observes of Sutherland, "is that you take the narration—the traditional narration of a folktale. In the course of the narration, you get a whole lot of dramatic behaviour which one should use, in writing plays even in English. . . . I believe with her that in order for African drama to be valid, it has to derive lots of its impetus, its strength, from traditional African dramatic forms."[1]

The agreement between Sutherland and Aidoo on this point is appropriate. As dramatists they both represent an approach to theater that is based on a marked concern with the relationship between the arts of theater (writing, production and acting, for example) and the very idea of tradition in a culture. At their best, their works exemplify a highly effective combination of Western stage conventions and African (that is, Ghanaian) traditions of oral literature and ritual folk drama. They also envision theater of this kind as an ideal symbol, or microcosm, of Ghanaian culture as a whole, in so far as that culture exemplifies the interaction of Western and African values. Since the dramatist's dramatic forms are themselves the result of this historical interaction, the play does not simply describe cultural traditions as such; the play itself and the theatrical process as a whole are part of the cultural interaction that they describe. In this sense, it is useful to approach this kind of theater as an extension of its culture.

Neither Aidoo nor Sutherland is unique in this perception of African theater as living social experience. The works of Wole Soyinka and John Pepper Clark in Nigeria clearly reflect an interest in the relationship between theater as dramatic art and theater as an example of the kind of cultural synthesis that these dramatists perceive in their society. But on balance, both Sutherland and Aidoo occupy rather special places in West African theater. More than any other dramatists of comparable stature they have been involved in the kind of theater that, as social microcosm, is specifically concerned with the significance of sexual roles and relationships in their culture. Clark's *Song of a Goat* and Soyinka's *The Lion and the Jewel* are equally specific in this regard. The breakdown of the marriage in Clark's work disrupts the family structure, threatens the stability of the community, symbolizes crucial changes and fluctuations within the culture, and, by implication, represents a disturbing instability in the moral universe. In *The Lion and the Jewel*, Soyinka presents Baroka's sexual schemes against the background of a changing society. The chief relies on traditional ritual and on folk theater as symbols in weaving his schemes, and in the process the sexual role-playing that he exploits emerges as a dramatic art (in terms of the theater itself) and as extensions of social convention. But Aidoo and Sutherland return to this issue far more frequently and consistently than any other playwrights in Africa, emphasizing the integral relationship between the conventions of sexual role-playing and the conventions of dramatic role-playing on stage. In the process they develop their dramas as the means of questioning and analyzing the meaning of convention or social tradition. At the same time, they also stress that the woman's experience is the central, or at the very least, the major, subject of their dramatic analysis.

The prominence of the woman's role is clear enough in frankly domestic dramas like Sutherland's *Edufa* and *The Marriage of Anansewa*. Even in the relatively nondomestic context of her *Foriwa*, which is primarily a political play, there is a significant link between the woman's sense of her own identity and her awareness of changes taking place in her society.[2] In these plays the woman's awareness of self and social tradition is interwoven with the manner in which the dramatist presents her theater as an extension of the woman's culture as a whole. In this regard, we frequently find that Sutherland draws unmistakable parallels between the ingrained habits of sexual role-playing and the artistic conventions of the theater. In other words, sexual roles and dramatic roles are analogous to each other, because both have evolved within and have been shaped by specific historical conventions—sexual roles by social conventions and dramatic role-playing by the conventions of the theater.

The conventions of the theater are themselves treated as a symptom of the manner in which social conventions—in this case, Ghana's—have blended new and old values, non-African and African traditions. Consequently, the pointed analogies between the idea of sexual role-playing and the idea of theatrical role-playing, in dramatists like Sutherland and Aidoo, have a crucial implication. They suggest that the issues of sexual identity and role-playing have been radically affected by the same complex process of cultural conflict and cultural synthesis that the theater itself reflects.

All of this implies a certain interest in theater itself as a direct social experience. There is an implicit philosophical concept here that is comparable with Francis Fergusson's thesis when he expounds on what he describes as the "idea" of theater: "If Hamlet could ask the players to hold the mirror up to nature," he observes of Shakespeare's play, "it was because the Elizabethan theater was itself a mirror which had been formed at the center of the culture of its time, and at the center of the life and awareness of the community. We know now that such a mirror is rarely formed." In a different kind of society from Shakespeare's, the "very *idea* of a theater, as Hamlet assumed it, gets lost. . . . We do not have such a theater, nor do we see how to get it."[3]

Fergusson's "idea of a theater" is rooted in the notion that whenever the conventions of staging and play-acting reflect fundamental social and philosophical attitudes, then the theater itself—all the trappings of dramatic *representation*—is literally a microcosm of the universe as the dramatists and their society understand it. In the case of the Elizabethans, for example, the very location and structure of the stage itself reflected the Elizabethan assumptions about the ideal social order, about human life, and about the significance, as well as location, of heaven and hell. In the middle, the stage itself represented humanity; above the stage the typical Elizabethan superstructure could represent heaven, while the traditional trap-door in the stage floor opened down into Hell. In other words, the physical structure of the stage itself was an immediate projection of the Elizabethans' moral and physical concept of hell, humanity, and heaven. The same structure simultaneously reflected an accompanying social hierarchy: the superstructure could represent the court and the ruling nobility, the stage itself could be the landed and trading classes below, while the trap-door opened down to the cellar of the menial classes (*The Idea of a Theater*, p. 14).

One senses that in Sutherland and Aidoo there is such a shaping, controlling idea of theater. In their hands theater in contemporary Ghana emerges as the amalgamation of new and old forms that have been drawn from both Europe (ancient and modern) and Africa (traditional and "Westernized"). In turn, this fundamental perception of the nature of their theater is inextricable from their perception of modern Ghanaian society as a mosaic of new and old, alien and traditional—especially as this mosaic is exemplified by sexual identity and role-playing.

Of the two playwrights the older, Efua Sutherland, has been deeply involved with the mechanics of theater production for years. This involvement has had a clear impact on her interest, as dramatic writer, in the nature of dramatic conventions—and in European as well as African contributions to these conventions. Sutherland received her early education in Ghana before attending college in

England. On returning home, she taught school in Ghana for some years and then launched the Ghana Society of Writers. In 1958 she established the Ghana Experimental Theatre, followed by the Ghana Drama Studio (for experimental productions). The Studio was subsequently incorporated into the University of Ghana's Institute of African Studies, and Sutherland herself has been a research fellow since then in the institute's School of Music, Dance, and Drama. In this capacity she has remained active in producing experimental plays and traditional theater, for adults as well as for children, promoting workshops that encourage writers and producers with interests in the relationship between traditional theater and contemporary Ghanaian life, and writing her own plays.

As writer, producer, and teacher, Sutherland has always been personally involved in the mechanics of theater, as well as the art of dramatic writing itself. Her career has enabled her to experiment with approaches to Ghanaian theater that explore the possible relevance of European models and the continuing vitality of indigenous folk drama and folktales. She has adapted Western drama (including her own adaptation of *Everyman*) to a Ghanaian context. At the same time, she has also been adapting Ghanaian tales to her contemporary theater. In fact, her career has been a "journey of discovery," to borrow her own words—a journey that has taken her from the adaptation of classical Greek drama *(Edufa)*, to the distinctive milieu of rural life in modern Ghana *(Foriwa)*, to the reliance on indigenous folk forms *(The Marriage of Anansewa)*. These are not the only plays by Sutherland. Her other works have included *Odasani* (the *Everyman* production), *Nyamekye* (a production of dance, music and speech), and some children's plays *(The Pineapple Child, Ananse and the Dwarf Brigade*, and *Two Rhythm Plays)*. But her three major, published plays exemplify at its best her continuing quest for certain dramatic forms—specifically, those forms which are analogous to the theme of sexual role-playing in the plays themselves.

In *Edufa* the classical Greek influence is represented by Euripides' *Alcestis*. As students of Greek drama are aware, Euripides' work is based on the legend of Admetus, king of Pherae, who has been doomed to death by Artemis for having offended the goddess. Admetus has been promised a reprieve if he can persuade someone to die on his behalf. After being rebuffed by other members of his family, including his parents, he accepts Alcestis' pledge to die in his stead. The grateful Admetus swears to remain a celibate after his wife's death. He promises her to give up his usual fondness for revelry—both vows being his assurance to Alcestis that he will mourn her for the rest of his own life.

Shortly after Alcestis dies Heracles, a friend of the family, pays a visit. Admetus is in a quandry at first. His responsibilities as a host do require him, as a matter of established custom, to entertain his guest, but this would mean breaking his solemn vows to his dead wife against revelry. He soon stifles his qualms and sets about entertaining Heracles. In return, Heracles undertakes to rescue Alcestis from death, and the play ends with her return as a silently mysterious figure who will only speak after a consecration period of three days. In Sutherland's play, death is not pronounced by an offended deity: Edufa simply learns that his death is imminent and that he can avert it by having someone die in his place. Edufa, a highly successful member of the nouveau riche, dupes his wife into taking his place by casually asking whether any member of his family loves him well enough to die for him. Ampoma says she does, thinking that she is responding to a purely hypothetical question, and in so doing dooms herself to death. Unlike Alcestis, her act of self-sacrifice is an unwitting one, but, like her Greek predecessor, Ampoma wrests the promise of life-long celibacy from her husband. Unlike *Alcestis*, Sutherland's play ends on a note of tragic finality: there is no rescue from death here.

The thematic differences between *Alcestis* and *Edufa* shed significant light on some of the implications of Sutherland's play. Euripides invests his characters and their motives with a highly effective ambiguity. He underscores the complexity of the human personality, especially in the moment of that ultimate choice between life and death. Admetus' selfishness and his cowardice in the face of death are therefore counterbalanced by the equal selfishness of those who decline to die on his behalf. In turn, the self-serving narrowness on both sides is weighted against the understandable instinct for self-preservation. Admetus demonstrates his fickleness and insensitivity by the ease with which he breaks his vow to the dead Alcestis by ordering revels in honor of the visiting Heracles.

But his hospitality is both a reflection of his genuine generosity and an observation of the strict laws of hospitality. As for Alcestis herself, the personality of the loving wife is matched by the inscrutable, even sinister, silence with which she returns from death; and the absolute selflessness which allows her to volunteer her own life for her husband's is equalled only by the ruthless single-mindedness with which she extracts from Admetus vows of life-long fidelity to her memory.

On the other hand, Sutherland's play prefers a less equivocal and more direct, satiric approach. Her Edufa is decidedly unambiguous, a grossly hypocritical man who is incapable even of the directness with which Euripides' Admetus requests his family to die for him. He represents a new breed that receives short shrift in the play, the new elite of educated and wealthy men who have adopted the worst features of Western culture (a cold-blooded materialism and a narrow individualism) and who demonstrate their "emancipation" by spurning African traditions of family, community, and religion, except in cases of emergency. Edufa symbolizes a debased and limiting notion of tradition: in his world the very idea of "tradition" has lost any connotation of the continuity of human values, and means simply the superficial forms that he has borrowed from the West and those few African conventions which he half-heartedly revives from time to time for his selfish needs.

Altogether, Edufa represents the moral anarchy that results from the rejection of a truly humane sense of society and its complex living traditions. It is significant, in this connection, that unlike Admetus, Edufa is offered an opportunity (by his father Kankam) to avert his wife's death by joining the entire family ("all of us whose souls are corporate in this household") in a collective beseech-ing of the gods (*Plays from Black Africa*, pp. 226-27). However, the selfish Edufa is too far removed from the traditionally communal values of family and religion, and he cannot respond to his father's appeal. Despite his shortcomings, Admetus has enough saving graces to merit his wife's reprieve from death, but when Edufa swears, in imitation of Euripides' Heracles, that he will force death to surrender up his wife, his futile threat is mere bombast: "I will bring Ampoma back. Forward, to the grave. . . . I will do it. I am conqueror. . . . Conqueror?" (*Plays from Black Africa*, p. 267).

Interestingly, Sutherland's work comes closest to the temper of her Greek predecessor's in the handling of Ampoma. Like Alcestis, Ampoma combines a capacity for loving self-sacrifice with a gentle but firm insistence on her own claims. She too exacts from her husband the promise that no other woman will share their children and their bed. As in *Alcestis*, the woman's frank self-interest implies a negative response to the husband's male selfishness. In this regard, Euripides' heroine is very skillful in the technique of using self-effacing devotion, not only as a genuine sentiment, but also as a firm, but covert, means of demanding her husband's respect.

This kind of claim is quite explicit in *Edufa*, especially when Ampoma reminds her husband that her impending death is really on his behalf, and that her love has been as self-destructive as it has been selfless. Her reminders to her husband and her claims on his fidelity seem to have a much more calculated effect than do Alcestis' demands on her husband in Euripides' play. This difference is largely due to the different circumstances under which the wives become sacrificial victims. In Alcestis' case it is a deliberate and informed act, taken with full knowledge of her husband's actual circumstances and the consequences for herself. In *Edufa*, however, the sincerity of Ampoma's offer to die on her husband's behalf does not really diminish the fact that she has really been duped into the role of sacrificial victim. In these circumstances, her reproofs to her husband imply a certain bitterness. In emphasizing the unselfish nature of her love, Ampoma is also subscribing to that strong sense of communal sharing which her husband has violated through his narrow selfishness and his greed. This is the same communality that her father-in-law invokes when he describes the family unit as a corporate body of souls.

Ampoma's invocation of the traditional ideals of a communal culture implies a certain sense of superiority to her destructively egocentric husband. In the process, she demonstrates that within this communal ideal sexual relationships enjoy a certain duality. They are a private, even intensely intimate, kind of personal sharing, but they are, simultaneously, a microcosm of that interdependence and sharing which is an intrinsical part of the communal tradition in society at large. It is therefore fitting that the chorus pays tribute, as it does, to these communal ideals when it comments on Ampoma's impending death:

Crying the death day of another
Is crying our own death day.
While we mourn for another,
We mourn for ourselves.
One's death is the death of all mankind.
(*Plays from Black Africa*, p. 234).

In Ampona's personality this sense of tradition is a creative force rather than a merely narrow preoccupation with established forms. Her mind is flexible rather than static, growing to meet changes in her world. Consequently, she is committed to the ideal of sexual relationships as the outgrowth and reflection of communal ideas—and in this sense she reflects a strong sense of tradition. At the same time she is committed to a certain notion of female individualism: she does insist on the woman's need for a less restricted role in the society. She is therefore at pains to describe her public display of affection for her husband as a new female individualism. Women, she declares, spend most of their time concealing, and therefore restricting, their capacity for feeling—"preventing the heart from beating out its greatness." In fact "the things we would rather encourage lie choking among the weeds of our restrictions." There is not much time left for women to act, she adds chidingly, addressing the chorus of women, but instead of acting on the need for this kind of frank self-expression, women "sleep" half of the time (*Plays from Black Africa*, p. 261).

This kind of forthrightness against female restrictions is quite unmistakable, even in the work of a writer who does not think too highly of being regarded as a woman writer. Indeed, this forthrightness is even underscored by making Ampoma's sentiments representative rather than unusual, for the chorus of women agrees with Ampoma's argument. They clearly accept her analysis of women's roles in their society as the kind of truth that most women, including themselves, agree with without having the courage to voice on their own. Many women, they observe at the end of Ampoma's remark, would like to be able to say what Ampoma just said (p. 261). By extension, their agreement with Ampoma's crucial analysis suggests that they do regard her death as the symptom of a certain problem—that is, male selfishness—in the lives of women in their society, in much the same way that they have come to see her death as a communal and universal event ("One's death is the death of all mankind").

Ampoma's personality represents a complex awareness of certain traditions in her society. She is able to perceive sexual love in conjunction with those communal ideals that have persisted into the present and which she wishes to uphold. At the same time she is committed to traditions, not simply as set conventions for their own sake, but also as a growing and responsive set of values. She prizes privacy, as well as the communal implications of her sexual love. As a woman she insists upon a certain degree of independence, without espousing the kind of individualism that subverts a communal life style. This degree of individualism conforms with the degree of change she accepts as part of a continuing sense of tradition; for her individualism is clearly influenced by the West while remaining in close touch, as Edufa's does not, with their African culture. Finally, her sense of individualism remains sufficiently communal to ensure that she speaks on the subject as a representative voice—who is endorsed by the chorus of women—rather than as an eccentric outsider.

That choral endorsement is also significant in another, related sense. It exemplifies Sutherland's habit of integrating a theatrical convention (in this case the chorus) with social conventions that affect sexual relationships and identity. The convention of the chorus, borrowed from the classical Greek tradition, has been combined with the social milieu (a contemporary Ghanaian town) of Sutherland's play. As such, it appears as a group of women whose songs and chants stamp their classically derived role with a distinctively Ghanaian character. This kind of adaptation is not peculiar to Sutherland and other African dramatists, of course. But it is significant in Sutherland's work because it reflects her interest in the way in which current practices in the theater may symptomize, even reenact, cultural adaptations in the society. As a synthesis of themes and conventions from ancient Greece, old Africa, and modern Ghana, the play *Edufa* blends dramatic traditions. In turn, this blending reflects the cultural synthesis that is taking place in the changing society of which the theater is a part. In effect, the changes in Sutherland's own society have inspired her "journey of discovery" for new, expressive forms, just as much as they have sparked Ampoma's search for an expressive individualism that is compatible with established but constantly evolving customs.

While Ampoma's experience represents the search for humane social forms, her friend Senchi is the artist who is bent on a certain quest for moral order and for the appropriate means of expressing that moral vision. Her friendship with Senchi, wandering poet and singer, reinforces the impression that both personalities are brought together in the play to function as a composite character. Senchi feels uprooted and alienated, and, as such, he is an extreme form of the muted restiveness which Ampoma reveals in herself from time to time.

Senchi's role in *Edufa* is roughly analogous to Heracles' in Euripides' *Alcestis*. Senchi is a friend of both Ampoma and Edufa, just as Heracles is a friend of Admetus and Alcestis. Both Heracles and Senchi are travellers who just happen to visit their friends at a time of crisis. The similarity ends here. Senchi is a perpetual itinerant. Unlike the ebullient and gregarious Heracles, he is alienated and often cynical. His alienation as artist is more than the effect of his own critical and questioning intelligence. It is also the outcome of dislocating changes in his society, changes which have uprooted the old African ways (respect for family, upholding of close-knit community ties, and so forth) in some quarters. Perpetual transient that he is, Senchi literally lives the experience of dislocation. Because he is repelled by the moral dislocations that he sees around him in the person of someone like Edufa, he is strongly committed to the idea of moral stability and to a social order that is stable while remaining flexible enough to accept orderly and humane change.

He shares this commitment with Ampoma. Therefore, her fate intensifies his barely concealed contempt for Edufa and for the new disruptiveness that is represented by Edufa's narrow selfishness and Western affectations. In Senchi's own words, both Edufa and himself make an odd pair, as friends, because Edufa's gross materialism is incompatible with Senchi's spiritual intensity as poet (*Plays from Black Africa*, pp. 246-47). Senchi's search for what he calls a kind and loving person (p. 238) is a quest for the kind of humaneness that could counteract Edufa's gross materialism. The circumstances of Ampoma's death represent another failure in that search. Her death means that he has ended up blank again (p. 268). Senchi's role in the play also bears upon the relationship between artistic form and the social themes of the artist. In a personal sense, his itinerant habits and ill-fitting clothes are symbolic forms, reflecting the dislocation and disharmony which his satiric songs and stories describe. His language and the narrative style of his stories and social commentary are usually incomprehensible to everyone around him, but that very incomprehensibility underscores the sense of moral breakdown and emotional confusion he sees around him in Edufa's home and social class. Finally, the inability of others around him to understand much of what he says emphasizes his profound alienation from society in general.

Senchi's role and personality are as integral to the hybrid nature of Sutherland's theater as is his friend Ampoma. As we have already suggested, Ampoma's personality is an eclectic one, and it conforms with the hybrid nature of the play's forms, themes, and social environment. In Senchi's case, we have a rather ambiguous personality. He is repelled by Edufa's shallow imitation of Western individualism and materialism. At the same time, his own eccentricities as an alienated intellectual reflect his Westernization; for the spectacle of a poet who is deeply isolated from his own society is a familiar Western image rather than a traditional role for artists in the old Africa. He cherishes the communal humanism of old Africa, and this preference is clearly indicated by his scorn for Edufa's individualistic materialism. At the same time, his Western-style intellectuality and alienation, as poet, make it all but impossible for him to communicate his ideas to the women of the chorus, the very ones in the play whose lives are relatively close to that old communal lifestyle. In effect, he is a personal example of the ambiguities and patterns of conflict described by the play's themes, and symptomized by its form. To borrow Fergusson's idea of theater, Sutherland's sense of her social milieu, her characters and her dramatic form blends perfectly with a prevailing pattern of ambiguities and adaptations, inside and outside her theater.

There is a marked shift of emphasis in the next two major plays. Sutherland relies less heavily on adapting Western and Ghanaian forms into a hybrid pattern in *Foriwa* and *The Marriage of Anansewa*. In these two plays, there is a greater emphasis on reviving a sense of old African traditions, or celebrating the ones that have managed to survive into the modern world. There is a corresponding shift away from hybrid theatrical conventions towards the indigenous forms and conventions of the dramatist's own culture. In fact, the themes and the staging of a work like *Foriwa* do not simply describe the revitalization of indigenous forms and values. The play itself is a part of this process of revitalization, for its very existence reflects a vital and continuing interest, among the playwright and her audience, in the indigenous forms.

As theater, *Foriwa* incorporates the folk rituals of the community's traditional African culture and, in so doing, the play imbues these forms and rituals with a fresh, contemporary significance. This is comparable with the manner in which its themes call for a renewed commitment to the substance, rather than mere form, of indigenous conventions. At the same time, the play's themes emphasize only those aspects of Western culture that are compatible with Africa's sense of its own traditions and with its place in the modern world.

The play is based on the same materials Sutherland uses for her short story, "New Life at Kyerefaso."[4] After years of neglect and local apathy, the town of Kyerefaso is visited by Labaran, a young university graduate who is determined to prod the community away from its narrow conservatism and from its obsession with local forms and customs for their own sake. Their conservatism, and general indifference to improving their community in any progressive sense have led, over the years, to economic decline and the deterioration of the school system. Labaran's objectives are similar to those of the town's Queen Mother, for she has been trying unsuccessfully, for years, to lead her subjects out of their apathy. Her daughter Foriwa joins forces with the queen and with Labaran, and their crusade for change is climaxed by the town's annual festival in honor of the river Kyerefa. The Queen Mother successfully transforms the festival from the usual parade of meaningless rituals into a ceremony that actually inspires the community to rebuild itself in the spirit of its original founders.

This transformation of the festival from empty rhetoric into a vital force for change is fundamental to the play as a whole. The Queen Mother does not break with the villagers' traditions as such.

Rather she insists that these traditions, particularly the annual ceremonies of birth and renewed life, become an actual experience in the life of the community itself. Thus, she mocks the traditional songs of praise to the ancestral founders of the town and to the river goddess, precisely because the present generation merely mouths the song while shunning the spirit of growth that it actually celebrates. The song has become a highly stylized and empty formality over the years, and the stilted style reflects the community's lack of spirit. The refrain promises that the singers will offer their "manliness to new life" in the river (p. 49), but Labaran, for one, is not convinced by the performance.

In his words, the river goddess should scream back a scathing response to the singers: "I am the lifestream of Kyerefaso. Your ancestors knew it when they chose to settle beside me. Are you going to do anything else besides dyeing my waters red from year to year with the blood of sheep?" (*Foriwa*, p. 35). When the Queen Mother repeats the traditional salute to the river-goddess, she transforms the language from a mechanical chant to a new and vibrant challenge: "Are your weapons from now on to be your minds' toil and your hands' toil?" she asks the men of Kyerefaso. "The men are tired of parading in the ashes of their grandfathers' glorious deeds. . . . They are tired of sitting like vultures upon the rubbish heap they have piled on the half-built walls of their grandfathers" (pp. 49-50).

In short, tradition ought not to be defined solely on the basis of a rigid loyalty to the achievements and symbols of the past. It should also incorporate a capacity for initiative and innovation, the kind of capacity that made the achievements of the past possible. The revitalized, direct language which the Queen Mother uses in her statement is part of a general revitalization (of forms, conventions, and language) which she perceives as integral to any living tradition. Since the prefestival ceremony at which she speaks and the rituals of the festival itself are forms of folk drama within the play as a whole, Sutherland has actually incorporated into her own theater the festival itself are forms of folk drama within the play as a whole, Sutherland has actually incorporated into her own theater the living, constantly renewed traditions of folk art. In effect, the structure and themes of the play exemplify the very principle that lies at the heart of the Queen Mother's argument. Traditional forms (folk art, in this case) are not simply antiquarian devices to be dusted off and used once a year; they should remain expressive and highly functional forms of communication.

The play's structure also depends on symbols and images that are integrated with the dominant theme of rebirth. These are drawn from the four-branched God-tree that dominates the town square and the setting of the play itself. The tree, near which Labaran has set up house, is actually described as a shrine. Its presence, throughout the play's action, is a highly visual example of what the Queen Mother and her allies are trying to achieve. It is old and a religious symbol and, on this basis, represents a very important link with the town's past. It is also alive and growing and, in this regard, it emphasizes the need to recognize traditions as living, growing conventions rather than static and antiquarian forms.

The tree's central location on stage, and its physical juxtaposition to the socially activist Labaran all have the effect of underscoring its significance as a symbol of social growth and change. At the same time, its religious significance reflects the degree to which social change should ideally be compatible with the deepest and most cherished of the community's religious and moral traditions. Finally, the "four-branched" design obviously emphasizes a sense of the universe (the four directions), indicating in the process that the tree's symbolism is both of local cultural significance and of universal implications. The kind of balance which Kyerefaso needs to strike between traditionalism and social growth is of immediate relevance to the community, to Africa as a whole, and to all cultures that hope to grow, and preserve their roots, in a changing world. By being located on stage the tree transforms the setting into a symbolic reflection of the community and the world view through which Sutherland presents the community. Given this centrality and dominance, the tree naturally makes its presence felt on the language of the play. Labaran describes himself and his mission as the scattering of seeds, in the manner of a forest tree (p. 34); and the Queen Mother herself exploits the tree image in defining custom as the "fruit" that the ancestors "picked from the living branches of life" (p. 25).

Significantly, this imaginative use of language and the capacity for growth which it represents, are also attributed to some of Kyerefaso's most apathetic residents, and in the process the dramatist hints at a dormant vitality, in the most unlikely society or individual, waiting to be released from static and unproductive notions of tradition. Thus, even the lazy draughts players who always ridicule Labaran's reformism are capable of a discriminating attitude towards expressive language, a sense of discrimination that bodes well for their ability to accept the challenges of expressive conventions in their community. The perpetual subject of Foriwa's beauty provides them with an opportunity to display the discriminating taste in language:

2nd Draughts Player. She only needs to show her face in at the door, and like palm wine, the flies come swarming after it.
1st Draughts Player. How crude, Butterflies after a flower is much more like it (p. 16).

The new life at Kyerefaso flows not only from the revitalized conventions of tradition and language, but also from the personalities and symbolic roles of the main protagonists—Labaran, the Queen Mother, and Foriwa. Labaran is committed to the idea of reviving decaying communities, by way of new schools, new libraries, and agricultural reform, and he represents what a new generation of Ghanaians and their education should be. He combines a strong reverence for the community's past with a desire to see it benefit from the more useful and humane elements of Western culture. He embodies the dramatist's familiar ideal, a perception of tradition as continuing customs that are constantly renewed by being exposed to contemporary experience.

Labaran is the creative traditionalist, opposed both to the slavishly Western Scholar's Union and to those who are narrowly faithful to the externals of Ghana's communal institutions. Conversely his alliance with the old bookseller in pressing for a new library and a new school involves the ideal union of the old and the new in creative views of tradition. Labaran is a Hausa "from the north" who is initially suspected as an outsider, but his commitment to Kyerefaso, and his eventual acceptance by the town, suggest that the redefinition and revival of local traditions must take place as part of the forging of a new and broader, but ideally inclusive tradition—the tradition of contemporary Ghanaian nationhood as a whole. At this point Sutherland's dramatic art exemplifies not simply the idea of theater but the idea of national theater.

Labaran's most powerful ally is the Queen Mother herself. Her office links her securely with the past and its heritage, but her commitment to contemporary needs endows her with an evolution-ary sense of tradition such as Labaran embodies. Throughout all of this, her identity as a woman is significant. Particularly on the basis of criticisms by older reactionaries like Sintim it is clear that the choice of a woman, and a literate one at that, has represented a radical departure from the customary method of choosing local rulers. Consequently, there is a significant link between the Queen Mother's views as ruler and the unusual fact that she is a woman who rules a reactionary community. She is not creative and pro-gressive simply because she is a woman. However, as a ruler she of-fers a creative vision and a capacity for innovativeness that cor-respond with the kind of flexibility that made her accession to power possible in the first place. As a woman in the role of public leadership, the Queen Mother is one of the play's two examples of the manner in which Sutherland has linked the question of social customs with the issue of the woman's role. The restrictive sexual conventions which Sintim recalls with longing, are based on the narrow and static modes of tradition that are choking Kyerefaso, just as the Queen Mother's accession and rule exemplify a socio-sexual liberality which is integral to the play's general emphasis on a progressive sense of tradition.

Foriwa is the second example of this sociosexual emphasis in the play. She is loyal to her mother's plans on behalf of Kyerefaso while demonstrating other levels of self-reliance and individualism. She is loudly determined to marry only someone of her own choos-ing, and, without being opposed to marriage as such, she remains detached from the mystique with which other women usually invest marriage. She has seen that for most of her married friends mar-riage has only been a dead-end which has dulled their eyes and slowed their "once lively" steps (pp. 6-8). Foriwa's active interest in marriage for herself (she is eventually betrothed to Labaran) and her capacity to criticize the stasis and narrowness that often afflict the tradition of marriage, all conform with that basic quality which she shares with Labaran and the Queen Mother, a deep respect for established conventions tempered by a critical awareness of the need to renew their meaning and form.

It is significant that Foriwa is assigned the leading role in the Queen Mother's formal challenge to the men of Kyerefaso that they give substance to their cherished customs. Foriwa is to dance with those men who are actually able to bring new life to the community. She declines to dance, on the ground that the men have not yet deserved the honor, but her refusal actually underlines the symbolism of the dance itself. It is a symbolic ritual, within the larger ritual of the festival and its preliminary ceremonies (such as the Queen Mother's challenge), and it represents the equal partnership of men and women in the (ideal) continuity of constantly renewed traditions.

The festival follows the confrontation between the Queen Mother and her foes. It is another symbolic ritual, for the eventual reconciliation between both sides is celebrated by the festival which represents the town's acceptance of her leadership and her challenge. They also accept Foriwa's role in all of this, for as a chastened Sintim remarks, Foriwa recalls the courage of those women who once made the ancestors men (p. 61). The symbolic celebrations of the festival are a prelude to yet another ritual, the impending marriage of Foriwa and Labaran. As a traditional ceremony, the marriage will confirm the continuity of established conventions. As the union of the two most innovative members of the community it celebrates the kind of progressiveness that must coexist with traditionalism.

On both counts, the impending marriage dramatizes the degree to which the new social experience envisioned by the play includes the ideal of sexual equality and independence for women as well as men. Finally, all of these conventions—the prefestival ceremony, the festival, and the impending marriage—are all forms of communal folk drama within the play. As a result, they allow Sutherland to integrate her vision of contemporary social changes with the continuity of folk art and folk traditions. Once again, her dramatic themes and conventions are a microcosm of the social order that she describes in her play.

The Marriage of Anansewa follows the direction of *Foriwa*. In this later play there is a succession of social conventions presented as forms of folk drama, and these combine to make the play itself a social microcosm. These conventions fall into two categories. One set relates directly to the art of dramatic narrative itself (that is, the communal tradition of storytelling), and the other set centers upon marriage.

Sutherland's introduction to the published version of the play dwells at length on the oral traditions of Ashanti storytelling, especially in the case of Ananse stories. As performances, these stories are a species of folk drama, allowing for audience participation. The audience participates through the Mboguo, musical interludes in which the performers add to, or comment upon, the main tale itself. This kind of audience participation enhances the function of the story as a form of communal art. Even more explicitly than in *Foriwa*, Sutherland is concerned with developing a kind of theater that is rooted in the established traditions of folk drama. The Anansegoro, as she describes this kind of theater, demands the ability of both dramatist and producer to invest the play with "some capacity for invoking this element of community participation" (p. vii).

The main plot of the play consists of the ingenious schemes through which Kweku Ananse secures money and other gifts from his daughter's suitors, encouraging each to send these gifts by leading him to believe that he is the favored suitor. Inevitably, the day arrives when all the suitors announce that they are on their way to meet Anansewa for a formal betrothal. Ananse averts disaster by announcing Anansewa's sudden death. All but one of the suitors send their regrets, in strict accordance with custom, but couched in terms which hint at difficulties that Anansewa might have encountered in their homes had the marriage actually taken place. The remaining suitor, Chief-Who-Is-Chief, goes beyond a literal adherence to the laws of custom. Since he has not been formally betrothed to Anansewa he is not obliged to assume responsibility for her "funeral," but he does precisely this, asserting the claims of husband on the sole basis of genuine feeling and loyalty. Overwhelmed by the Chief's generosity (not to mention his wealth), and released from his dilemma by the withdrawal of the other suitors,

Ananse promptly announces the miraculous return of Anansewa from death, and the play ends with Anansewa's betrothal. Her marriage to the chief is in the immediate offing.

Within the structure of Sutherland's Anansegoro, the storyteller is both narrator and spectator, using the Mboguo to comment upon Ananse's schemes for the benefit of Sutherland's audience —while at the same time functioning as on-stage audience. This dual role underscores Sutherland's play-within-a-play structure. In turn, this structure contributes to the kind of audience involvement that is demanded by the Anansegoro format, for the resulting impression of multiple action and multiple audience has the total effect of blurring the usual distinction between stage and audience, action and detached spectator. Ananse as schemer is really a perpetual actor whose schemes are witnessed, at first hand, by a selected audience—the storyteller himself. Then, in turn, the storyteller's relationship with Ananse's plots, as well as the plots themselves, comprise that overall dramatic plot—the "play"—that Sutherland's audience witnesses. Finally, this all has the effect of strongly implying that the theater as a whole, including the audience, is part of a larger theater—society—with its own patterns of social roles. Sutherland's idea of theater (as the extension or microcosm of social conventions and role-playing) has become clearly interchangeable with a certain idea of society (as a theater of traditionally defined roles).

Given this broadly representational nature of the play's action, it is appropriate that Sutherland conceives of Ananse himself as an "Everyman" (p. v). He is the consummate actor on this Ghanaian version of the world stage, spinning and acting out a succession of plots like the legendary Spider God after whom he is named and upon whom his character is based. He is the perennial trickster, well versed in the art of deception, and an expert without peer in the business of social intrigue and domestic plotting. His art of deception is therefore both an analogy and an integral part of theater itself, for dramatic art is really a convention of hoaxing an audience that is already predisposed to be deceived, and to be instructed in the truth by way of deception.

In the process, Ananse exemplifies the manner in which the theater is an extension or direct expression of the individual's personality and the individual's social experience. If his skills as a plotter and trickster reflect his personal greed and ambition, then the economic necessities that also contribute to this ambition reveal much about his immediate social conditions and the human condition in general—the condition of Everyman-Ananse. Therefore the song ("Oh Life Is a Struggle") which ushers him unto the stage also introduces the theme of adversity that justifies his schemes, at least in his own eyes. In his words, "While life is whipping you, rain also pours down to whip you some more. Whatever it was that man did wrong at the beginning of things must have been really awful for all of us to have to suffer so" (p. 1). Ananse's appeal to our sense of human history and to our awareness of traditional human suffering is important here. He is deliberately linking the moral justification of the trickster's role with the idea of tradition, claiming, in effect, that there is an intrinsic connection between his art as trickster and the history of human adversity.

His talents as actor are varied, ranging from an acutely discriminating use of language to his knowledge of established social conventions. The letters with which he flatters and cajoles money from the suitors are carefully composed in the long established, ego-massaging techniques of the praise-song. They are also shrewdly tailored to conform with the rules of courtship and marriage. His language is therefore generally encouraging, without offering the specific promise or undertaking that, according to the established custom, might commit Anansewa to any one of the suitors. The letter to the chief of Sapa is typical in this regard:

Since forwardness has never been one of my faults, I will
not even dare to drop a hint that the way is open for you now
to begin oiling the wheels of custom. You who do not pay mere
lip service to law and custom but really live by them, need no
prompting from anyone.
    Therefore I will only add that I'm very happy to be,
Yours in the closest of links in the not too distant future (p. 6).

As the storyteller remarks, it is clear that Ananse knows the customs very well (p. 16). Like the storyteller himself, Ananse judges others on the basis of their knowledge, and practice, of established customs. Thus, the final choice of a suitor for Anansewa is really made to depend on each suitor's attitude towards the appropriate customs of courtship, marriage and mourning. The ideal suitor is expected to know the customs, but he is also expected to use them in a flexible and humane way. Chief-Who-Is Chief is clearly the winner because he fits this ideal. He does not allow personal feelings of love and generosity to be thwarted by an overly literal attention to the conventions of courtship, betrothal, and mourning. On this basis, the chief represents the familiar Sutherland ideal of a flexible and creative traditionalism.

All of this brings us to the second group of conventions comprising the heart of the play—conventions that deal with marriage and other social institutions. Here Anansewa is a central character. Unlike her father and future husband, she is relatively inexperienced in the ways of the world and in the conventions through which one organizes, or copes with, those ways. An ingénue of sorts, she is really drafted by her father into his schemes before she is fully aware of his objectives. Her marriage is important in the play, not simply as an event towards which the plot is moving, but also as a process—or rather the culmination of a process. This is the process of education, her education. She has to be initiated into the ways of her world through a succession of conventions and rituals which represent certain experiences or values and which are to be climaxed by her impending marriage at the end of the play.

The first of these conventions is a formal education in certain Western skills that are necessary to modern society. Therefore, she is a trained secretary. Her secretarial role in her father's schemes (she types his letters to the suitors) initiates her into the formalities of traditional courtship—and in this regard she is yet another Sutherland character who combines the modern with the traditional. After her father announces her "miraculous" return from "death," she undergoes the "outdooring" ceremony. The ceremony is a necessary preliminary to her betrothal. It formally marks her growth into womanhood, establishing her as a debutante of sorts. It is part of a step-by-step education of a young woman in the traditions of her culture, including the tradition of marriage.

As a symbolic initiation into adulthood, that outdooring ceremony is also complemented by the ruse of her fake death. Followed as it is by the life-oriented ceremonies of "outdooring," betrothal, and marriage, her mock-death becomes, in retrospect, a ritualistic reminder that death itself, and the conventions that attend it (mourning, funeral, and the responsibilities of family and suitors) are intrinsic to life itself. In other words, Anansewa's growth as woman combines the customary patterns of initiation into adulthood with a growing awareness of harsh realities—like her father's poverty and death itself.

It is therefore appropriate that Ananse's schemes are interwoven with the conventions through which Anansewa is initiated into womanhood. She is thereby assured of an initiation or growth which is not simply based on a set of rituals observed for their own sake, but which imbue traditional patterns of womanhood (father's daughter growing into husband's wife) with an urgent awareness of life as a struggle. This process also endows her with a vital sense of her own personality and choices. Thus, she refuses to countenance her father's schemes if they were to bind her to a husband whom she would not choose.

Her education, like that of the audience itself, has proceeded through the hoaxes and disguises of Ananse's plots. In this respect, she is a highly personalized symbol of the way in which Sutherland's theater functions: she both reflects and experiences the social conventions of the audience's world. At this point Sutherland's social vision and her interest in the woman's role and identity have merged. They have become the central focus of her idea of theater.

5   Ama Ata Aidoo

Among contemporary Ghanaian dramatists, male and female, only Ama Ata Aidoo compares with Sutherland in exploiting oral literature, especially folk drama, in modern theater. Like Efua Sutherland, Aidoo has taught extensively in her field. She graduated from the University of Ghana in 1964, and subsequently attended a creative writing program at Stanford University in the United States. Since then she has taught as a research fellow at the Institute of African Studies in the University of Ghana, and as visiting lecturer in other African universities and in American colleges. Both as writer and teacher she has always demonstrated a special interest in the kind of oral literary traditions that so strongly influence her own plays.[1]

As Aidoo has remarked, her ideal form of theater is one that capitalizes on the dramatic art of storytelling. This kind of theater, she feels, would actually be a complete environment in which the usual amenities of eating and drinking would be combined with storytelling, poetry-reading, and plays (*African Writers Talking*, p. 24). In Aidoo one encounters a trememdous confidence in the integrity and inclusiveness of the oral tradition. She perceives the tradition of storytelling as one that actually combines techniques and conventions that are often separated into distinctive genres, especially in the Western literary tradition. The storyteller's art is therefore a synthesis of poetry, dramatic play-acting, and narrative plot. This art is social in the most literal sense. The artist is physically and morally located in the center of her, or his, audience, and the story itself reflects and perpetuates the moral and cultural values of the audience. Consequently when Aidoo talks of a theater that, ideally, duplicates the oral tradition, she is emphasizing the inclusiveness of that oral tradition—and the extent to which the art and function of the storyteller's performance become direct extensions of the storyteller's society.

Aidoo's first play, *The Dilemma of a Ghost*, is a fairly obvious example of this ideal at work, for it is closely associated with a distinctive storytelling tradition. This particular tradition is now known as the dilemma tale. The dilemma tale usually poses difficult questions of moral or legal significance. These questions are usually debated both by the narrator and the audience—and on this basis the dilemma is a good example of the highly functional nature of oral art in traditional Africa. William R. Bascom has recognized this feature in his collection of dilemma tales from several areas of Africa, including the Akan region in Ghana:

They are prose narratives that leave the listeners with a choice among alternatives, such as which of the several characters has done the best, deserves a reward, or should win an argument or a case in court. The choices are difficult ones and usually involve discrimination on ethical, moral, or legal grounds. Other dilemma tales, which border on tall tales, ask the listeners to judge the relative skills of characters who have performed incredible feats.

. . . . Like many other African folktales, their content is often didactic, but their special quality is that they train those who engage in these discussions in the skills of argumentation and debate and thus prepare them for participating effectively in the adjudication of disputes, both within the family or lineage and in formal courts of law.[2]

Bascom is quite correct in emphasizing the adjudicative function of the dilemma tale. The simple fact of posing a question is not the special feature of this kind of tale. It is the manner in which the questions are posed, for it is not necessarily assumed that the questions themselves can be answered, or that the underlying moral and legal problems can be solved. The raising of such questions and the debates that they provoke really function as a kind of intellectual exercise that develops and continually stimulates the audience's ability to discuss such dilemmas in everyday experience. It is therefore not difficult to see why such a storytelling tradition would attract someone like Aidoo with her strong interest in drama as an extension of the folktale heritage. The explicitly functional context of the dilemma folktale is compatible with her frank interest in the social setting of contemporary theater. The raising and debating of questions in the dilemma tradition is an example of the way in which her ideal theater would itself be an extension of the audience's society: that is, theater should raise issues that are of immediate and pressing relevance to the theater-goer's experience.

In *Dilemma of a Ghost* the central problem or issue is presented as a play-within-a-play. A boy and a girl play the game, "The Ghost," holding hands and skipping in circles as they sing the ghost's story. The story is a simple one: early in the morning, while the moon was still shining, the singers went to a crossroads, Elmina Junction. There they saw a "wretched ghost" debating with himself: he was trying to make up his mind which road he should take—the one leading to Elmina itself, or the one to the city of Cape Coast (pp. 23-24).

This vignette is presented as a dream by the boy, now grown into the young man, Ato. Ato, the play's main protagonist, is really the "ghost" of the play, for he is incapable of making firm choices in a society where fundamental changes often pose crucial questions. He himself represents some of those changes, having been sent to the United States for a university education. The circumstances under which he returns home are not easy. His family, having underwritten his education at great expense, has great expectations of the returning scholar. The black American bride with whom he returns is quite controversial because of cultural differences between Eulalie and her in-laws, and Ato contributes to the difficulties by not being frank to either side—by failing, for example, to explain to his family the nature of certain decisions (such as birth control) which he and Eulalie have made.

Eventually, it is Ato's family that demonstrates the ability to deal humanely and flexibly with a complete stranger whose ways are alien and whose ignorance is often compounded by arrogance. At the conclusion, Ato the scholar is literally deserted on stage, still unable to demonstrate any capacity for the complex choices and for the kind of compromise that are required by the conflicts between

old and new ways—between the culture of an older generation of
Ghanaians and the new modes that are represented by his own wife,
his education, and his civil service job.
   The tradition of the dilemma tale has been absorbed, not only into the play's themes by way of the dream-sequence, but also into
Ato's personality. His character has been presented according to
the basic principle in the art of the dilemma tale—the posing of
ethical and sociopolitical choices and the individual's ability to
weigh and make those choices. The audience's reaction to his
character is therefore determined by the manner in which Ato fails
to cope with the problems which have been formally presented by
the play's dilemma-tale design. In assuming the ethical motives of
the dilemma folk tradition, the dramatist's art has also adopted
some of the characteristics of that design.
   The ghost's dilemma is not only presented within Ato's consciousness (by way of his dream), thereby emphasizing the tale's
immediate psychological pertinence. It is also presented in the communal context of the oral tradition to which it belongs (by way of
the children's play-song), thereby juxtaposing Ato's dilemma as a
contemporary Ghanaian with the communal customs which insist
upon the need to deal with moral and social dilemmas. This kind of
juxtaposition is as important to the play's structure as it is to the
characterization of Ato himself, for the play brings together the
distinctive literary conventions of different cultural traditions (the
Ghanaian and the European). The formal five-act structure incorporates the folk vignette of the ghost's tale upon which it draws for
its central theme, and in the process the European convention of
act divisions becomes the theatrical context for the ethical viewpoint and communal mode of Aidoo's oral tradition. Similarly the
familiar chorus assumes a double identity, recalling the interpreta-
tive functions of the standard Western chorus and revealing in its
dialogue structure (between two women) the unmistakable colloquial rhythms of living speech in Aidoo's Akan culture. The narrative embellishments and judgements of the chorus are offered
from the vantage point of concerned neighbors, and they constitute
the kind of communal perspective that is brought to bear on the
alien individualism of both Ato and Eulalie.
   Take, for example, the women's news of Eulalie's rumored
pregnancy:

2nd Woman: As for you, my sister!
              She uses machines.
              This woman uses machines for doing everything . . .
1st Woman: But this is too large for my head
              Or is the wife pregnant with a machine child?
2nd Woman: Pregnant, with a machine child?
              How can she be?
              Does she know what it is to be pregnant
              Even with a child of flesh and blood?
1st Woman: Has she not given birth to a child since they married?
2nd Woman: No, my sister,
              It seems as if the stranger-woman is barren.
1st Woman: Barren?
2nd Woman: As an orange which has been scooped of all fruit (pp. 34-35).

The dramatic conventions upon which the play is structured reflect Aidoo's diverse cultural sources; and taken together these sources represent the multiple choices that are integral to Ato's dilemma and, by extension, to his changing society as a whole.

The role of women in one of these conventions, the chorus, is not unique, but it is appropriate here, for as women the chorus embodies and emphasizes the domestic or family context within which the play's dilemmas are located. More specifically, their role as commentators in the chorus and their identity as women bear directly upon the fact that the woman's situation is a focal point in the dilemma themes of the play. In describing Eulalie as the product of a machine-culture, the women speak out of a cultural tradition to which Eulalie is a complete stranger and from which she is progressively alienated when she is confronted with its expectations of a woman as wife and mother. On one hand, the rather brutal history which has often fragmented the black American family has given Eulalie a strong incentive to become part of the closely knit Odumna clan into which she has married. On the other hand, her American upbringing and the cultural habits which it represents, result in her being hostile and incomprehensible to Ato's family. In one sense, she is the outsider, amusingly naive at best and intolerably arrogant at her worst, but, in another sense, she is the archetypal New World black in search of West African roots and, through those roots, a coherent sense of her ethnic identity. In this cultural conflict, which is clearly analogous to Ato's dilemmas, her identity as a woman is of immediate significance. Her individualism scandalizes the communally oriented women of Ato's family just as much as her decision against childbearing for the time being. Her dilemmas as a woman (a sense of obligation to Ato's family versus her own egotistic preferences) are explained by the fact that she is a non-African woman as well as by her black American self-conflicts.

In keeping with the complexity of choices which she inherits from the tradition of the dilemma tale, Aidoo does not offer a simple contrast between a confused Eulalie and a simple, monolithic image of African womanhood. The Ghanaian women in the chorus demonstrate conflicts, or a sense of alternative possibilities, which are intrinsic to their own situation as African women—especially on the issues of childbearing and motherhood. The First Woman is childless, and she repeatedly bemoans the misfortunes of women like herself (p. 5) while recalling the wisdom of the ancestors in extolling the virtues of motherhood (p. 16). The Second Woman, whose house is teeming with children, envies the childless woman's freedom from this "curse," as she describes childbearing.

The relative advantages of childlessness and childbearing are therefore as open to debate in the experiences of these women as they are in Eulalie's different cultural context. Of course, the parallel is not complete. Despite her complaints about her own fertility, the Second Woman does not really repudiate the maternal role as such. On the whole, one does not detect in her situation the kind of free choice Eulalie exercises in the matter—much to the scandalized amazement of Ato's mother, Esi Kom: "I have not heard anything like this before. . . . Human beings deciding when they must have children" (p. 48). Moreover, even in her most outrageously selfish moments Eulalie's general image of untrammeled independence wins a reluctant admiration from Esi Kom herself, especially when Eulalie refuses to accompany her husband to a traditional thanksgiving festival. In Esi Kom's words, "I would have refused too if I were her: I would have known that I can always refuse to do things" (p. 48).

Ultimately, the family crisis generated by Eulalie's presence is resolved, not by any clear-cut choice or pat solutions by Eulalie or Ato, but by Esi Kom's recognition that Eulalie's failings have been due to the natural errors of a stranger compounded by Ato's bungling and indecisiveness. Just as she recognizes some enviable qualities in Eulalie's independence, Esi Kom also perceives that the women of the community may have contributed to the conflict with Eulalie by virtue of their ignorance of Eulalie's world. Esi Kom's real assistance to the younger woman lies in the fact that the former recognizes Eulalie's dilemmas as a displaced black American and as a woman caught between conflicting cultural assumptions about women. Neither Esi Kom, nor the play as a whole, really claims to have solved the complex dilemmas of Eulalie's identity and Ato's personality. In this regard, the play is comparable with the dilemma tale, posing questions which are not necessarily accessible to easy, straightforward solutions and which, by their very complexity, ensure a crucial recognition of the complexities of social relationships and individual feelings. What is important here is the fact that Esi Kom is able to offer the kind of compassionate understanding that her son lacks, and that the older woman, unlike Ato, has the perspicacity to recognize her own ignorance as well as another's.

Much of the traditional wisdom which Esi Kom embodies and which is inherent in the play's dilemma conventions is rooted in a frank self-knowledge—the candor with which the women of the chorus reveal a certain ambivalence towards childbearing and motherhood in a society that prizes children, or in the honesty with which Esi Kom herself can admire Eulalie's individualistic sense of choice even at the very moment that the older woman deplores the crude arrogance of that individualism. Ato and Eulalie, on their side, represent and experience the dilemmas of a new generation of Africans and black Americans, both in terms of broad cultural choices and with specific reference to domestic relationships and sexual roles. On the other hand, Esi Kom and her contemporaries represent the kind of wisdom traditionally demanded and nurtured by the convention of the dilemma folktale: as the principal agent of reconciliation and compassion Esi Kom's personality integrates the traditional insights of the oral convention with the moral perspectives of the play as a whole. At this point, in a perspectival as well as structural sense, Aidoo's theater literally becomes an extension of the oral tradition.

The plot of *Anowa* is more indebted than that of the first play to oral literature. In *The Dilemma of a Ghost*, much of the plot is based on original materials cast in the conventions of the dilemma tale. In *Anowa*, the narrative as a whole is based on a legend the playwright heard from her mother and which was based on historical events in nineteenth-century West Africa (*African Writers Talking*, p. 23). Moreover, there is a more direct and urgent attention in this second play to the problems of sexual roles and identity as they affect men and women. The story is set in the 1870s, approximately thirty years after the Bond treaty with the British opened up the door to European hegemony in the Fanti area of what was then called the Gold Coast. After declining several offers of marriage approved by her parents, Anowa elects to marry Kofi Ako, an impoverished but ambitious young man of whom her family disapproves.

As a result of the rupture with her family, Anowa leaves home, traveling and working with her husband as he amasses a fortune as a trader. Kofi's greed increases with his success, and with it an exploitive selfishness which progressively alienates Anowa—especially when he outrages her moral sense by acquiring slaves. Eventually, she publicly humiliates him by charging that his neglect of her has been a means of masking his sexual impotence, because he has "exhausted" his "masculinity" in acquiring slaves and wealth (p. 61). The disgraced Kofi commits suicide and Anowa then drowns herself. The tragic ending and the charge of sexual impotence which leads to it, are Aidoo's own additions to the original legend. They have the effect of emphasizing the analogy between Kofi's loss of humanity in the pursuit of wealth and his loss of sexual potency (*African Writers Talking*, p. 23).

The historical events which Aidoo interweaves with her legendary materials are also important in the play's themes. In recalling the Bond treaty which bound the Fanti to British rule, the old man of the prologue introduces the familiar theme of change, encouraging the audience in this case to recognize links between the arrival of an alien and hostile culture and the cold-bloodedness of a new generation represented by Kofi. The moral problem represented by Kofi is not entirely the result of change as such. Hence, the prologue offers pointed reminders about the complicity of an earlier generation in the arrival of colonialism (by virtue of having signed the Bond treaty) and less excusably, in the trans-Atlantic slave trade. In the words of the old man, the Bond treaty could at least be justified by expediency, by the need for allies against aggression from the north, but there has been a "bigger crime" which has been inherited from the past, and which is commemorated by the (slave-trading) forts on the coast (p. 6). The inhumanity which leads the greedy Kofi to own slaves is a part of the brutishness that flowed from the Bond treaty and its consequences, but it also represents the continuation of a long-standing "crime" in Kofi's society.

Aidoo's themes imply a social continuity in systems and traditions. This thematic definition of social history as a recognizable continuum, with evil as well as good implications, is comparable with Buchi Emecheta's fiction. It is particularly apt in this play because it complements and reinforces her dramatic structure. The historical precedents cited by the prologue have been succeeded by those specific events and judgements (involving slavery, for example) which link Anowa's world with its past, and, in turn, the legend of Anowa has been incorporated into the moral insights and the design of Aidoo's drama.

In effect, the dramatist's art is centered in that continuity which characterizes not only history itself but also the tradition of oral art which re-creates and interprets that history. The play has been integrated with a historical sequence that begins with the conventions and historical events of the past, continues with the legend which interprets that past and its relationship with another generation, and culminates in the play's re-creation of the entire process. As the old woman of the chorus remarks at the conclusion of the play, "This is the type of happening out of which we get stories and legends" (p. 63). The same impression is created by the repeated references to the fact that Anowa behaves like those heroines in tales who refuse to marry solely out of deference to their parents' wishes and who are individualistic (pp. 7, 64). This all has the effect of avoiding precise, antithetical distinctions between historical "fact" and legendary "fiction," emphasizing, instead, the continuity of moral truths that are inherent in the succession of historical events, the legends which they inspire, and the contemporary theater which duplicates that continuity by way of theme and structure.

A major effect of that duplication consists of the manner in which the tragic experience is intensified by the very impression of continuity, even permanence, which the play's design attributes to the individual and collective "crimes" of society. This is most notable in Kofi's character. His ambition to own slaves is both the effect of his greed and the symptom of an obsession with power. On both counts he is tragically representative of human history. The language with which he attempts to justify slavery to Anowa also links him with those white slave owners and colonizers whose oppressive presence has been synonymous with the black bondage that preceded and followed the Bond treaty: What evil lies, he asks, in having bonded men as laborers (p. 37)?

His amassed wealth includes possessions which demonstrate the degree to which he has become the colonial heir to Western civilization. He owns a large house equipped with a useless and rather incongruous fireplace, for example. The furnishings include a large picture of Queen Victoria. Kofi's fascination with power is not limited to his obsession with the trappings of Western slavery and colonialism. His power-hungry ego also takes the form of a narrowly conservative masculinity. Very early in his marriage he is uneasy with Anowa's strong self-confidence, and he tends to be upset by her obvious determination to have her individual views respected. After she insists that he take a second wife to share their labor and criticizes his use of medicines and taboos, he muses ominously, to himself, that his wife has a few "strong" ideas. Thenceforth, his relationship with Anowa is based on his resolve to subdue her to his will and to wield unquestioned authority. According to his scheme of things, he will be a new (assertive) husband and she will be a new (submissive) wife (p. 27).

The connection between Kofi's masculine authoritarianism and European colonialism is quite clear in the play. They are both examples of oppressive and exploitive power. Similarly, the play illuminates the psychological links between his identification with European imperialism, and his need to dominate his wife and to own slaves. On both counts Kofi suffers from an almost pathological need to exercise power, and to identify himself with symbols of power. There are noteworthy parallels between Aidoo's play and the fiction of Nigeria's Adaora Lily Ulasi. Ulasi's two novels strongly imply some connection between entrenched male privilege, on one hand, and established patterns of power, on the other hand

—in both African society and the European imperial system. Like Ulasi, Aidoo establishes this link without necessarily arguing that the problem is a peculiarly or exclusively *male* one. Although the distinguishing norms of male behavior are stamped with a male preoccupation with power, the real issue is that power has become a corrupting and destructive force in both cultures simply because the power-brokers have entrenched themselves on exploitive and narrowly selfish grounds—not because they are males as such. Power-brokers, who happen to be male, have been corrupted by the basis and nature of their power rather than by their male identity. Because neither Ulasi nor Aidoo defines the problem is an exclusively biological sense, it is possible for us to find humane potential in the occasional male who strays from the established power norms in Ulasi's fiction. Conversely, one of the most ferocious upholders of the status quo in *Anowa* is the old woman of the chorus, Mouth-that-Eats-Salt-and-Pepper.

By a similar token, the women in Ulasi's fiction and women like Aidoo's Anowa are capable of a certain detachment from, even hostility to, traditional power, not because of some peculiarly female perspective as such, but because as traditional victims of power they are more sensitive to its abuse. Their intimacy with the traditional wielders of power makes them very aware of the real insecurities and unstable needs that are masked and served by the male's preoccupation with seizing and exercising power. As Anowa herself muses, the man's insecurities, his fears of seeming weak, usually require that the woman subordinate herself to him so that he can be a man, that is, be strong (*Anowa*, p. 52).

At this point, of course, Aidoo is not simply linking the male's passion for power with historical precedents in African and European history. Kofi's personality and conduct are also an extension of established social customs in his own time and place—especially those customs which shape sexual roles and relationships. He is comparable with Anowa's father, Osam, who has been as uncomfortable with her independent spirit as her husband now is. Osam has always held that her family should have apprenticed Anowa to a priest in order to quiet her spirited individuality (p. 11). Anowa's mother, Badua, is horrified by Osam's suggestion, one that he repeats shortly before Anowa announces her engagement to Kofi. But in reality, what Badua objects to is not the idea of a subdued, conventionally submissive daughter. She simply does not think that being a priestess is the proper or profitable way of being a human or normal woman. Priestesses, she reminds Osam, do all kinds of odd things—communing with spirits, jumping into fires, and feeding on dog's eyes and goats' blood. Her Anowa should be more conventional—marry, tend a farm, bear children, and accumulate enough property to earn her a respectable place in their society (p. 12).

The point of the play is not that the roles outlined by Badua are oppressive or limiting in themselves. The real issue as it so often is among women writers from Africa, is the need for more freedom in electing to adopt or reject such roles. There is something essentially oppressive about the manner in which men like Kofi and Osam, or women like Badua, assume that only certain roles are acceptable as the criteria for a fulfilling and respectable womanhood. In the process, they refuse to accept the legitimacy of attitudes and roles that do not meet their criteria.

Men like Osam and Kofi are predictably insecure and domineering when they argue on behalf of a limited notion of women's roles or choices. On the other hand, there is a pathetic sense of personal inadequacy in women like Badua who accept this imposed limitation by declaring that a good woman is one who lacks a brain and a mouth (p. 33). The deep roots of this conventional acceptance are demonstrated by the age of one of their most vociferous supporters —the old woman of the chorus. The loquacious Mouth-that-Eats-Salt-and-Peppter unmistakably echoes Badua's definition of a good woman at a crucial junction in the play. Anowa has just futilely objected to Kofi's plans to buy slaves, and the old man who forms the chorus with the old woman, has just defended Anowa's stand by commenting on the evil of slavery. In response the old woman angrily denounces Anowa as an evil creature, a devil and a witch who probably came into the world as a cancerous tumor rather than as a normal child. The witch reference is spiteful and potentially dangerous for Anowa since witchcraft is a capital offence in her culture, but the old woman is also emphasizing the degree to which Anowa's independent spirit is unnatural in a woman. Anowa is abnormal in her tendency to act as if she knows better than her husband, for she is ignoring one of the cardinal laws of sexual relationships and sexual role-playing: "The dumbest man is/Always better than a woman./Or *he* thinks he is!" (pp. 40-42).

In spite of her hostile manner, the old woman's language does suggest a certain detachment, even subversiveness. Her emphasis ("*he* thinks . . . ") clearly implies that the superiority of the dumbest man to any woman is not necessarily an indisputable fact but may simply be a matter of what the man believes, or needs to believe. This male belief is particularly crucial for an understanding of how women like the old woman and Badua perceive their roles and their relationships with men. There is a certain ambiguity about the woman's acceptance, or apparent acceptance, of male superiority. On one level she is obviously acquiescent: the man's alleged superiority is unchallenged, at least on the surface. On another level there is a covert but quite strong strain of scepticism.

This scepticism is exemplified by Badua's personality. Her claim that a good woman is one who is stupid and silent fits the ideal image of female subordination, but Badua's good woman is not only stupid and silent, she also manages to acquire considerable property and prestige by way of marriage and hard work. If Badua is a representative example of her own ideal, then a good woman is not necessarily silent. Badua is anything but silent and self-effacing. She contradicts and harangues her husband quite frequently and freely. Far from being stupid she obviously perceives and uses an apparent submissiveness as a device through which conventional, married women like herself can be materially successful without arousing the fears and jealousies of their husbands. Consequently, when she demands that Anowa adopt the traditional role of sub-missive daughter and wife, Badua's arguments are cleverly calculated to equate submissiveness with profit and respectability.

In effect the established norms of male power have bred a cor-responding, and equally destructive, preoccupation with power among women who accept the status quo. Among women like Badua, that acceptance really amounts to a calculated form of manipulativeness which effectively circumvents the man's insistence on unquestioned male authority, by using submissiveness as a mask that allows them to gain and exercise their own power. In the final analysis, this covertly subversive and manipulative exercise of power is as morally questionable as the man's open authoritarianism. Consequently, Kofi's domineering maleness and Badua's scheming submissiveness are both sides of the same coin. The man's frank need to dominate is matched by the woman's covert drive for power of her own. Badua's approach to the issue of power and sexual roles is as indefensible as Kofi's—notwithstanding the fact that women like herself really develop an obsession with power in response to the man's domineering role. Her reliance on connivance and covert manipulation is understandable as an age-old tactic of resistance and survival by some women. But this kind of tactic is morally limited because it really depends upon the maintenance of the status quo rather than upon a full commitment to the humanization and complete equalization of sexual roles. It therefore never really develops into a forthright condemnation of the male dominance to which it is reacting. Indeed, it actually requires the perpetuation of that dominance. In the process it fails to raise ethical questions about the use and abuse of power itself.

These are precisely the kinds of questions that Anowa is able to raise—because she is so genuinely alienated from the ways in which both men and women manipulate and exploit each other: "I hear in other lands a woman is nothing. And they let her know this from the day of her birth. But here, O my spirit mother, they let a girl grow up as she pleases until she is married. And then she is like any woman anywhere: in order for her man to be a man, she must not think, she must not talk" (p. 52). Her open rebelliousness is free from the moral defects of her mother's covert power-plays. In their own thirst for power Badua, and women like her, are just as ruthless as their men. In the process they really condone and perpetuate morally defective conventions of power in their public and private lives, in their past, and in their present. On the other hand, Anowa's aversion to exploitive patterns of power is open and complete, ranging from her spirited opposition to slavery to her continuous determination to remain independent. She declines to accept the notion, fostered by her husband and her mother, that there are inherent, and unequal, differences between men and women, finding instead that they all live in a world in which they are all wayfarers, belonging "to oneself without belonging to a place" (p. 36).

She is the quintessential wayfarer, an independent person who, as her husband complains, is always "looking for things" (p. 28). Her general restlessness is partly explained by her quest for the means of guaranteeing her independence as a woman. It is also a symptom of that ethical energy through which she establishes her moral integrity, in opposition to her husband's deficiencies. This is also the moral energy which enables her to perceive the woman's situation as the symbol of African history—a history of slavery, colonialism and repressive power that seems to be crystallized in the image of the African woman as slave mother:

> I dreamt that I was a big, big woman. And from my insides were huge holes out of which poured men, women and children. And the sea was boiling hot and steaming. And as it boiled, it threw out many, many giant lobsters, boiled lobsters, each of whom as it fell turned into a man or woman, but keeping its lobster head and claws. And they rushed to where I sat and seized the men and women as they poured out of me, and they tore them apart, and dashed them to the ground and stamped upon them. . . . Since then, any time there is mention of a slave, I see a woman who is me and a bursting as of a ripe tomato or a swollen pod (pp. 46-47).

Anowa's crusade against entrenched abuses does not mean that she opposes tradition as such. In fact she can be quite insistent on the need to observe certain customs—polygamy, for example— whenever she feels that they serve humane purposes. All of her significant actions and judgements are rooted in the assumption that humaneness and moral integrity are the crucial lessons to be derived from a full understanding of history. She is comparable with the old man of the chorus who criticizes both the old woman and Kofi by appealing to a certain sense of history. He is the one who recalls the earlier precedents of slavery and colonialism as examples of persistent patterns of abusive power which are now embodied by men like Kofi and women like Badua.

His sympathies for Anowa are based on his recognition that she has been true to herself (p. 64). That is, her respect for history and tradition has not been blindly servile, or narrowly self-serving; it has been the kind of insightfulness which has sustained her in- dividuality and nurtured her moral integrity, enabling her to derive humane values from the lessons of the past. Consequently, if Kofi and the old woman are traditionalists in the narrow and suspect sense of repeating the errors of the past, then Anowa and the old man represent another kind of historical continuity. They embody the persistence of humane perspectives on the problems of power and identity in their culture. Taken together, both sides reflect the essential ambiguities of history itself, which is a continuous succession of events, legends and conventions that depend upon the individual capacity for humane wisdom or abusive power. In effect, both sides constitute the process, intrinsic to the play itself, of interpreting and responding to the continuum of social history.

Aidoo practices the art of theater as a direct extension of social conventions, particularly of those conventions which are intrinsic to her oral traditions. Her theater, like Sutherland's, represents a strong commitment to oral literature as a complete and complex tradition in its own right. Not surprisingly, Aido disagrees "totally" with those who "feel that oral literature is one stage in the development of man's artistic genius. To me it is an end in itself." In her view, there is no reason why theater should not simply consist of the rendition of oral art on its own terms (*African Writers Talking*, pp. 22-23).

Theater as social and artistic tradition therefore derives much of its legitimacy in Aidoo and Sutherland from the manner in which it duplicates and incorporates the conventions and insights of the oral forms. These dramatists are concerned with that concept of theater in which the dramatic art, like the art of oral literature, will be experienced and judged on the basis of its integration with both established and changing social customs. In this sense, theater as a living tradition does not depend on those familiar criteria of permanence and fixed meanings which are often offered as the only significant characteristics of "major" literature. This view of theater is more consistent with the oral artist's custom of combining a sense of permanence with a process of continual change.

By immersing herself in the oral tradition as much as she has done, Aidoo has become acutely aware of the distinctive contributions that the oral form offers simultaneously to several genres. She recognizes the degree to which the art of an oral performance may incorporate poetry, drama and narrative prose. Consequently, her

interest in theater as an extension of the oral tradition is complemented by her even greater activity in the short-story form. In
this regard, she tends to view the short story in much the same way
that she views the theater, and the oral tradition with which she
associates both genres. Her short stories are conceived as performances—oral performances: "I pride myself," she has remarked,
"on the fact that my stories are written to be heard, primarily"
(*African Writers Talking*, p. 24).

In Aidoo's hand the short story is a literate medium, drawing
upon the Western conventions of the genre. It is also an intrinsic
part of the writer's oral tradition, drawing upon the dramatic
modes, the narrative techniques, and the communal customs of the
oral artist. It is necessary to emphasize the degree to which Aidoo
seems to be aware of what she is about in her short stories, because
the limited criticism that her work has attracted so far already includes the dubious claim that she has not mastered her form, and
that her storytelling art is marked by random shifts in viewpoints
—shifts that are allegedly "clever" rather than useful.[3]

Curiously enough, this kind of criticism is actually useful in a
perverse sort of way, because it pinpoints one of Aidoo's distinctive strengths as a short-story writer. She is painstakingly attentive to the relationship between form and narrative viewpoint,
on one hand, and characterization or theme, on the other. Viewpoint and form shift in order to match the personalities and experiences of her characters. Since she conceives of each story as an
oral performance, the language of each story is carefully adjusted
to conform with milieu and theme. Although this basic strategy
arises from her indebtedness to the oral tradition of her own culture,
it is also very much in evidence when she chooses to write about a
Westernized milieu with standard English and with Western literary
conventions.

Each Aidoo story bears the idiosyncracies of her protagonist,
and reflects the manner in which each protagonist is conceived as a
performer offering judgements and justifying actions by way of a
personal performance. Thus, even in a rare Aidoo poem we can see
her consistent strategy as short story writer at work. For example,
in "Last of the Proud Ones" the language is carefully subordinated
to the powerful personality and voice of the old woman who speaks
in the work. As the last survivor of her generation, she is con-

temptuous of the new-fangled ways, and the strange inventions, of the modern (Westernized) world. A diet of bread and cheese is therefore an unspeakable abomination, and she will have nothing to do with it. The stuff, she snorts, "reeks, reeks/the odour of stinking fish!"[4]

It is important to emphasize that Aidoo consistently applies this technique—the short story as oral performance—to all of her short stories, irrespective of whether or not they are drawn directly from the nonliterate milieu of her rural characters or from the literate and literary traditions of Western narrative forms. This consistency suggests that she is able to apply a method that she cultivates out of her own oral tradition to a modern, literate medium. This ability is significant because it represents an achievement that is often discussed but rarely achieved in African literature—the integration of traditional oral techniques with Western literary forms.

There is a significant diversity of techniques in her stories. Colloquial rhythms reflect rural Fanti life styles; colloquial forms and standard English are juxtaposed to dramatize cultural conflicts or cultural integration; and a uniformly Western style reflects Western attitudes or, Western insights into the nature of female roles, in both traditional Africa and contemporary Western societies.[5]

"In the Cutting of a Drink" exemplifies the first category. The oral framework complements the age-old rural background of the male narrator, and the title itself establishes the communal ritual which envelops the story-teller's art within the oral tradition. The cutting (that is, the pouring) of a drink is the narrator's reward and incentive in the telling of the story. The storyteller's occasional break from his narrative to call for his drink ("Cut me a drink, for my throat is very dry, my uncle. . . . ") serves a multiple purpose. It heightens the dramatic suspense of the narrative, since this thirsty self-interruption usually occurs at crucial points of the story. The call for a drink emphasizes the orality of the narrator's art, both in a literal sense and in the implied reference to the physical nature of his medium ("my throat is dry").

The call for a drink also affirms the communal implications of the narrator's art by claiming the storyteller's due reward for a communal service. The total effect of this communal emphasis is the heightening of the reader's awareness; we are now impressed with the importance of moral and auditory relationships between the traditional values of the audience and the narrative techniques of the storyteller. He is a young man in a rural village describing to his elders the strange lifestyle of the modern, Westernized city which he has recently visited in a search for his sister Mansa who had left home twelve years before. His audience represents those family values and sexual mores which are alien to the ways of the city, for the city the young narrator has experienced is characterized by the disturbing, yet excitingly exotic nightclub, that most urban of Western imports, with its iron chairs and tables, women who drink beer like men, and couples dancing in ways that he cannot (that is, will not) describe (*No Sweetness Here*, p. 34).

He eventually does describe how they danced, and how he danced with the "bad" women of the city in that night club. He also details the appearance of these women—their long, straightened hair (like that of white women), their red, painted lips, and their provocative, skin-tight dresses. His gradual relaxation throughout his narrative not only allows him to speak of the (hitherto) unspeakable; it also represents the gradual shift of his moral viewpoint from a complete identification with the old rural mores towards an ambivalent awareness of the city and its "bad" women. One of the women, the one with whom he dances, turns out to be his sister. She rejects his brotherly solicitude and his rural morality. Significantly, his resigned declaration at the end of his story echoes his sister's rebelliousness. There is nothing to worry about, he assures his family with self-pitying sarcasm:

"I was sent to find a lost child. I found her a woman.
Cut me a drink . . .
Any kind of work is work. . . . That is what Mansa told me with a mouth that looked like clotted blood. Any kind of work is work . . . so do not weep. She will come home this Christmas (p. 37).

The verbal echo of Mansa's defiance suggests that the once naive storyteller seems to have understood something about her world of city prostitutes. His search for Mansa turns out to have been his own quest for worldly wisdom, and the discovery of his sexuality in the "liberated" atmosphere of modern Accra. The maturity of Mansa, of which he is so acutely aware, is analogous to his own experience. To paraphrase his words, a boy was sent to find a child, and a man found her a woman. The narrator's own growth is implied by the shift of narrative judgement and style from the tentative, even reticent, naiveté at the beginning of the story to the boldly stated observations at the end. This acquired ability to perceive the sexual ways, and roles, of the modern urban world is underscored by that repeated cutting of drinks: the alcoholic bravado suggests a kind of celebration of growth.

However, this acquired perception or understanding does not involve a total acceptance. The celebration of that knowledge about the world and about his own maleness arises from his contact with the adult urban woman, but it does not mean that he has broken away from the old traditions of his village. That final demand for the cutting of a drink reaffirms all of those moral and communal relationships which the call implies between storyteller and audience. It is as much of a celebration of the village tradition as it is a celebration of his new knowledge and sexual maturity. This new knowledge tempers his inherited conservatism, hence, the repeated echoes of Mansa's liberated work ethic is neither exclusively condemnatory nor sympathetic. It is both pitying and self-pitying, gently mocking and at the same time tinged with sexual regret.

He and his rural audience have been exposed to a new order that seems, incomprehensibly, to flourish beyond the well-defined boundaries of village and custom. Despite the ambiguous effects of that exposure and despite the imminent arrival of that new order in their midst (in the form of Mansa's promised Christmas visit), the old order of clearly defined sexual roles and familiar customs lives on—for the time being at any rate. The cutting of a drink, both as social event and narrative art, celebrates that continuing, though precarious, order of things in which the woman is still her mother's daughter rather than her own bad woman, in which mother and daughter function within the cohesive structure of a homogenous family unit and extended communal family, and in which the artist and his storytelling art are still organic parts of the communal experience.

The focal point of all this is the woman's role. The urban woman's relatively unrestricted sexuality arouses the male narrator's possessive puritanism, while at the same time it stirs the erotic self-consciousness which challenges that masculine puritanism. The archetypally "liberated" woman of the city represents a broader cultural challenge to the older order from a brash, alien life-style. If the coherent family structure (which is emphasized by the narrator's asides to uncles, brothers, and his mother) represents a stable, conventional tradition, then the "bad" women of the city are symbols of a new uprootedness that is both exhilirating and destructive. Above all, the woman of the city bears a radically subversive image precisely because she can no longer be perceived or described within a conventional family context. She is no longer a woman of the family and, quite apart from the morality of her sexual and economic choices, this uprooted condition is bad (that is, disturbing and menacing) from the settled communal viewpoint of the old order. The ambivalence with which Mansa's brother views her world is shaped by that communal viewpoint, especially with regards to the subtle incest themes of the story. His sexual attraction to the young woman with whom he dances in the night club is largely explained by the seductiveness of the strange life-style that she represents and by the frank, alien sexuality that she offers, but the incest-taboo quickly squelches this attraction when she turns out to be his sister. All of this has the effect of emphasizing the degree to which the settled customs and traditional morality of family and community are being threatened by a new world that is both alluring and forbidden. They are both enhanced by the promise of a strange individualism and fraught with dangers for the older community.

In "A Gift from Somewhere" the oral background of the short story once again represents those "set" patterns of an older African order. Here, the traditional society is aware of an alien world on its borders, particularly as this strange world is perceived by the woman herself—in this case, the rural woman. Mami Fanti's situation is familiar enough in the context of rural family life. She has already lost two children to sudden, mysterious illnesses, and now her third child is dying. These background details are quickly outlined in the opening dialogue between Mami and the holy man (the Mallam) whom she has summoned to save the child. Additional information in this vein is supplied by the Mallam's (sceptical) thoughts about the child's condition.

When the narrative shifts to a detailed analysis of Mami's own situation, there is a corresponding shift to the distinctive cadences of Mami's own speech—the colloquial rhythms of "Afro-English" with which Aidoo reproduces the texture of her characters' spoken

(African) language. Here Mami's style is the medium through which the story examines her roles as mother and wife. After the Mallam's visit she reflects on those roles as she prepares for the worst—the death of her child and the resumption of what appears to be an endless succession of pregnancies and child deaths. It seems, she thinks bitterly, that she was created only to be pregnant for nine months every year, but, she decides resignedly, this is something that she will have to get used to, because it seems to be the "set" pattern of her life (p. 81).

Mami's stoical reserve towards childbearing contrasts with the popularity of motherhood, especially in a society that measures the prestige of a woman by her ability to have children. Mami's rather unquiet desperation really implies a certain restiveness, albeit covert, regarding conventional expectations of her as woman. Notwithstanding that note of fatalistic acceptance, the restive tone influences the reader's (and her audience's) response to the monologue which constitutes the rest of the narrative. The monologue opens several years later when we overhear her celebrating her child's recovery. Her language recalls the lavishly effusive style of traditional "praise" oratory: "But you know this child did not die. It is wonderful but this child did not die. Mmm. . . . To his day name Kweku, I have added Nyamekye. For, was he not a gift from God through the Mallam of the Bound Mouth?" (p. 81). Not only did this child recover, but she has not lost any children since his illness.

This enthusiasm about the gift of her son's life confirms her sense of womanly fulfillment as a mother. In this regard, her triumph counterbalances the earlier signs of rebelliousness, but it is placed in an ironic context. Despite Mami's effusive gratitude to the absent Mallam, and despite her faith in his powers, the fact is that the Mallam himself has always doubted Kweku's ability to survive. The holy man's candid sense of impotence in the matter therefore undercuts Mami's gratitude to a divine source for the gift of motherhood, and the impression is that motherhood may not necessarily be blessed with all the divine sanctions in which she professes to believe. Her rhapsodies about being a mother do not augment her audience's faith in the notion of motherhood as a sacrosanct and totally fulfilling duty. On the contrary, the ironic context of her rhapsodies creates the impression that this is really an indirect expression of that earlier impatience at the "set," traditionally defined patterns of her role as a woman. In a manner of speaking, Kweku is her way out from the traditional pattern. His future offers her a vicarious means of breaking out by way of the Western education that will remove him from a traditional rural lifestyle. Thus, as she explains to her enraged husband, she does not wish Kweku to perform the customary chores on the farm because he is growing up to be a scholar and not a farmer.

Kweku has become an alter ego for Mami Fanti, one which reduces the significance of the father's world (she never mentions him by name) by vicariously projecting her into that other world with which Kweku's Westernized future is associated. Conversely, the father has adopted the habit of describing Kweku and the other children as *her* children, that is, as the carefully cultivated projections of Mami's restive personality. Mami's total absorption with Kweku is also a means of compensating for what she sees as the limitations, the "set" patterns of her life. She makes this compensatory motive quite clear when she reflects on her husband's puzzling (or so she claims) resentment of Kweku. She does not care about his resentment, for she has her children (p. 85). When she looks at a reminder of her husband's resentment (a scar on her arm) she blots this out with a certain image of Kweku. Her son's miraculous survival confirms her womanliness in the conventional, maternal sense. He is also the focal point of her muted, but continuing, impatience at the limitations of her own life. Whenever she sees that scar on her arm she is glad it is not on her son, rejoicing at the same time that the Mallam had saved him from death (p. 86).

This points to an interesting ambiguity in Mami's character and her awareness as a woman. Motherhood is not only a symbol of what she regards as restrictive patterns, it is also the means whereby she can triumph in her achievement as woman within the definitions established by those patterns. She is therefore both rebellious and conforming, raising questions about the customary role of women whenever it is a burden for any reason, but quick to exploit it in order to revel in the customary ideal of female accomplishment. She is both ingenuously subversive and deliberately conventional—ingenuous enough to claim, with an air of convincing sincerity, that she is puzzled by her husband's resentment, but remaining loyal enough to established customs to claim the prestige which they confer on her as a mother. Although there is an aura of calculated rebellion in her use of Kweku as an alter ego and in her covertly subversive enjoyment of motherhood, she remains sufficiently committed to the conventional roles of wife and mother to be unaware (publicly, at any rate) of the full implications of her own rebelliousness.

Even after allowances are made for her ingrained sense of tradition, her rebellion should not be seen merely as an unconscious subversiveness. Her disclaimers about the possible cause of her husband's hostility seems too calculatedly innocent—they seem to be all part of an ingrained habit of using pretended ignorance as a means of self-protection and subversiveness. Her loyalty to the status quo continues, but it does so in a state of conflict with her other, less accepting identity. This conflict takes the form of a contrast between the alien new ways of the West and the traditions of old Africa, but it is not limited to a clearcut antithesis between the old and the new, between African civilization and Western culture. Mami's self-conflict is also based on established (Akan) norms of motherhood, and it should be noted that her dissatisfaction with being wife and mother actually precedes her vicarious "liberation" by way of Kweku's imagined future as a Westernized scholar.

Therefore, quite apart from the impact of an alien culture, Mami's restlessness in her social role also reflects the familiar tension between the individual will and the prevailing cutoms of social traditions. In effect, the private self-conflict has been aggravated rather than inspired by the shadowy Western presence in the story. Viewed in this light it suggests that the role of the woman, as exemplified by Mami, has always existed in her society in the state of a perpetual, but dynamic and potentially creative tension between the community's ideal of womanhood and the woman's occasional rebellion against that ideal—even in the very moments in which she affirms a genuine loyalty to them.

Both "In the Cutting of a Drink" and "A Gift from Somewhere" suggest a sense of conflict, within the culture, about the woman's identity and role. In the latter story Mami's personality makes this conflict a highly individual issue, largely because of the continuing confrontations between herself and her husband. This personal feud raises questions about the man's role in the woman's perception of herself. Mami's husband emerges with the image of a capricious man who is capable of malicious violence, and even after allowances are made for the biases of the narrator (Mami herself), the story as a whole implies that the woman's dissatisfaction with her role is partly caused by some shortcoming on the man's side. This criticism of the man's role remains vaguely insinuating rather than fully developed in "A Gift from Somewhere," largely because Mami is really an ambiguous rebel and because her split loyalties to both new and old ideas of womanhood do not permit her to offer straightforward and unequivocal criticisms of her husband and his role. However, the discussion of the man's role is more explicit and unambiguous in two stories which are presented wholly through the oral modes of traditional folk literature: "Certain Winds from the South" and "Something to Talk About on the Way to the Funeral."

The hostility towards the male is clear in "Certain Winds from the South," but it is softened by the primary emphasis in the story on those social changes, in nothern Ghana, which have crippled his effectiveness. The narrative is presented from the viewpoint of old M'ma Asana, widow of a former cattle herder whose son-in-law Issa is about to leave the barren cattle lands of the north, his wife, and his newborn son in order to seek employment in the south. Issa's decision is particularly painful to the old woman because it recalls the night, several years before, when her own husband left her with a young child to join the army in the Second World War. M'ma Asana's love and longing for her husband have survived his death in the war, but so too has her bitterness at his decision to abandon her in order to fight on behalf of those very "Anglis-people" who have occupied the lands of her people. His enlistment had been motivated largely by the usual masculine need to excel among other men, even at the cost of deserting his family and aiding his people's colonial enemy.

On balance, it appears that M'ma Asana is criticizing her late husband on two grounds. She faults him for having neglected those family responsibilities that have been decreed by their customs, especially since this kind of neglect by the men has contributed to the decline of their families and the community as a whole. She is also critical of those male shortcomings which have been due in part to external changes—the war which drew the men from the grazing lands to the cities of the south, the disruptive presence of the English colonizer and its impact on customs of family responsibility and communal unity, and the perpetual cycle of death and life which has brought crippling drought and famine to the northern region. All these have contributed to a process of change in which the man's traditional role as leader and provider has decayed, and with that decay women like M'ma Asana feel particularly vulnerable both to the familiar capriciousness of the male ego and to the relatively new order of things that seems to be located in the perennially attractive, pervasively influential south.

Aidoo's choice of the old woman as her principal narrator is as effective as the choice of a young man as narrator in "Cutting of a Drink." The young man as narrator naturally invests Mansa's urban lifestyle with an image that is as attractive to his male sexuality as it is disturbing to the family unit to which he remains loyal—thus far. In "Certain Winds from the South" M'ma Asana's age allows her to convey a highly effective sense of contrasts and parallels between the present and the past. She sees her dead husband in her son-in-law, in that the latter is also responding to outside pressures. Unlike her late husband, her son-in-law has no real choices (the younger man is driven by desperate economic need rather than by a narrow male selfishness). This contrast between the two men compels M'ma Asana to recognize that those social changes, which were once symbolized by the strange military uniforms of an earlier geneation, are now more decisive and destructive in her world.

Altogether the old woman as a narrator represents a historical viewpoint on the nature of social change—both as an immediate impact on family roles and as part of a perpetual, universal pattern of life and death. As an old *woman*, her awareness of her own body allows her a highly personal experience of that universal pattern. She recalls that the women's pregnancies were once followed by births, then by deaths. Now that the women were rarely pregnant, the life-death cycle has been broken: without pregnancies there were no more births and, ironically therefore, no more deaths. Then her womb "moves" upon reflecting that her grandson's birth has been the first in twenty years (pp. 47-48).

M'ma Asana's awareness of her body is as crucial to her perception of history, family, and sexual roles as are her age and experience.

As she tells us, she perceives through her womb: her womb felt the news of her husband's death twenty years before (p. 54). This female body-consciousness dominates the narrative style, as much as her actual language. It inspires that sense of the life-death cycle which is so concrete and personal to women whose customs emphasize the sacrosanct and necessary nature of childbearing.

The old woman's physical understanding of change makes her sensitive, in a deeply personal way, to the impact of change on the old order. She remains loyal to that order, perpetuating the mystique of the *male* birth and emphasizing in her own person the preeminence of family and womb in the old tradition. Given her personal closeness to the recurrent realities of change she is also capable of a sympathetic understanding in the face of certain changes. The criticism of her husband's desertion is tempered by an awareness that he and his generation were moved, however unwittingly, by disturbing and uprooting changes in their world. By a similar token, although Issa's departure saddens her by recalling those earlier desertions, her age and experience have instilled an awareness of that continuity of things which survive change. Even the disaster of Issa's departure cannot negate the need to continue to cope with recurring necessities—market days, food for dinner, and so forth (p. 55). M'ma Asana is a study in the survival of women from an older generation in a world which has changed drastically in their lifetime. Without even being as restive as Mami Fanti, she is frank enough about what she sees as disadvantages as wife, widow, mother, and now grandmother in a world of threatening changes and unstable or limited men.

"Something to Talk About on the Way to the Funeral" is another study in woman's capacity to survive. The woman in this case is Auntie Araba whose funeral serves as the narrative background. Her story demonstrates the vulnerability as well as the strengths of women in both Westernized and traditional African societies. To be more precise, this is really a summary of Auntie Araba's life. As the young servant to a "lady" relative she becomes pregnant by her employer's husband, and is sent home quietly in order to save the relative's marriage. Her son Ato grows up to be a "big scholar" who, in turn, fathers a child by a young woman in the village. Auntie Araba takes in Mansa (the young woman) and the child after they had been expelled by Mansa's parents. Both women live together as mother and daughter with a thriving bakery business while Ato studies at an overseas university, with the understanding that he will marry Mansa on his return. Ato subsequently breaks his promise in order to marry into a powerful and wealthy family whose daughter he "had gotten into trouble." Mansa leaves to work in the city but Ato's treachery and Mansa's departure are too much for the aging Araba who dies shortly afterwards.

Throughout, there is some rather frank criticism of the men in Auntie Araba's world. They have been invariably irresponsible, tending to abuse privileges which have accrued to them because they are male. On their side, the women who narrate and analyze Auntie Araba's life on the way to her funeral see woman as victims of male selfishness and arrogance. They trace the vulnerability of Auntie Araba and Mansa to be privileged selfishness of "big" educated (Westernized) men like Ato and to "big" men in the traditional mold (such as Araba's first lover). Women, as one of the narrators exclaims, deserve to be pitied (p. 122). But if these women think that their situation is pitiable, they refuse to be self-pitying. Instead they emphasize the strength of will and purpose which allowed Auntie Araba to survive and and transcend disasters, qualities that have been inherited by the level-headed Mansa. In the final analysis, the funeral both mourns the sexual inequities which beset women like Auntie Araba in town and country, and celebrates the resiliency with which these women of rural backgrounds cope with their vulernable situation.

Appropriately, this celebration of strength-in-weakness draws upon a ceremony (the funeral and its conventions of tribute to the dead), as deeply rooted in the oral tradition as the storytelling form with which Aidoo's narrators describe their rural experience. Like the funeral the story unfolds as a dramatic pattern. The narrators are both spectators and storytellers, insinuating their own experience and judgements into the story of Auntie Araba's life, and functioning in this regard as the chorus of the theater. This has the effect of establishing a tightly communal context by virtue of the narrators' multiple roles—storytellers, audience, participants, and choral commentators. In the other stories that are written in an oral frame of reference, the emphasis is on the individual's (male or female) perception of the community and its sexual traditions.

Here, it is the individual woman who is the object of the community's scrutiny by way of that highly concrete, communal context which Aidoo establishes through her narrators. This communal perspective is continuous throughout the story. The omniscient narrator does not appear, and the dialogue between the two gossips is uninterrupted by any third-person commentary. Apart from the obvious fact that they are from Auntie Araba's village, the precise identity of the *individual* narrators remains undiscovered, thus reinforcing the communal significance of their storytelling role. Auntie Araba's story is being told between friends, members of the same community whose experiences and sympathies are shared with Auntie Araba and her kind. They are the community that they describe. To be brought into the storyteller's confidence is to have one's communal standing confirmed, not only as a member of the wider community, but also as a woman with problems of vulnerability and survival that are shared by the other women—and this is precisely what happens at the beginning of the narrative dialogue when one of the narrators (who has been away from the village temporarily) has to be brought up to date on the latest events in Auntie Araba's life.

The act of narration is an act of confirming the general community ties and special female links between narrators and their audience. The story is therefore interrupted from time to time in order to ensure that there are no uninvited listeners. The narrative technique is not simply a storytelling skill but is also an intrinsic part of the narrator's sense of community—the woman's community within the larger social group. On the other hand, there is a pointed emphasis on the reader's role as an uninvited outsider from a literate and literary background. The reader is the invisible eavesdropper who is literally listening in on the community's collective views about an individual woman, her close ties with the traditional community, and her links (as well as the community's) with that other society represented by the reader's literacy.

In her second group of stories, Aidoo makes fuller use of non-oral modes, juxtaposing them with oral techniques in order to suggest the dual perspectives of men and women in a changing society. The oral and non-oral forms come into conflict with each other in "The Message," and the conflict reflects the contrast between two value systems. The title refers to the telegram which

(Nana) Esi Amfoa receives from the city informing her that her granddaughter has had a caesarean section. Quite apart from its reference to the communications system of a technological culture, the title also connotes the oral medium which dominates the old woman's world and which shapes the theme and style of the story from the beginning:

"Look here my sister, it should not be said but they say they opened her up."
"They opened her up?"
"Yes, opened her up."
"And the baby removed?"
"Yes, the baby removed."
"I say . . ."
"They do not say, my sister."
"And how is she?"
"Am I not here with you? Do I know the highway which leads to Cape Coast?" (p. 38).

The patterns of statement and repetition come together to form a carefully integrated whole: the dialogue becomes an oral symbol and expression of the communal integration of the speakers' world —the world to which Esi Amfoa belongs and which is so different from the city hospital that sends the telegram. Her inability to comprehend the idea of a caesarean section emphasizes the gulf between the two worlds. Those two worlds come together in the lorry which takes her to the city to visit her granddaughter. The vehicle and the transportation system of which it is a part are repugnant to the old woman (they are alien and reek with petrol), but the vehicle also acquires a communal atmosphere from the decidedly oral disposition of its users, from the constant exchanges between passengers and driver, and the steady refrain by the passengers, "O, you drivers."

Once Esi reaches the hospital, the narrative is dominated by the language of urban technology and European culture. Here Esi is merely an ignorant old village woman in the eyes of the nurses. The communications gap is complete, ironically reversing the ideal of communications implied by the title of the story: the nurses know of no Esi Amfoa (Esi's granddaughter) and the old woman does

not know the patient's European name. However, in spite of the
indifference and contempt with which the world of technology and
urban culture regards the villagers, it does concede a grudging admiration for the hardiness of Esi and her kind. The physical strength
and courage which the doctor admires in the granddaughter becomes a general symbol of the toughness and resilience which
characterizes the older Esi, and all of the older rural women of
Aidoo's work.

The fact that grandmother and granddauther share the same
name lends credence to this symbolism. Notwithstanding her disadvantages in relation to the alien urban world and those problems
which are inherent in her rural world, Aidoo's rural woman enjoys
a strength and a capacity to endure which Esi Amfoa and her granddaughter exemplify. Young Esi's survival of the awesome hospital
and its dreadful operations assures the older woman that this
strength has remained unabated: her only "pot" has refused to
"get broken" (p. 46). It is significant that in these concluding
statements, placed in the mouth of the old woman, the story has
returned to the language and viewpoint of the village; for the final
dominance of Nana's style and perspective confirms the author's
tribute to her strength and courage. Neither is this tribute developed
sentimentally. It is one of Aidoo's consistent strengths that she is
able to evoke strong sympathies for the rural woman without
minimizing or glossing over her limitations or disadvantages. In
Nana Esi's case, the understandable ignorance of the strange city
heightens our awareness of the woman's vulnerability in the new as
well as old order. But there is no mistaking where the author's (and
the lorry-driver's) sympathies lie in this confrontation between
Esi's world and the supercilious new breed of self-satisfied literates
(particularly the nurses) who deride Esi's ignorance without recognizing her humanity and strength.

The relationship between the literate elite and the unlettered folk
is more productive in "For Whom Things Did Not Change,"
primarily because the educated person in the story (a young doctor)
makes a real effort to bridge the gulf between his Western middle-
class world and the world of his cook. Here the two distinct viewpoints, those of the doctor and his cook Zirigu, come together as a
double perspective that reflects the dual nature of modern African

cultures—partly rooted in the older African values of Zirigu and his world, and partly embracing new ideas from Western culture. The relationship between the two men becomes more personal and less formal as the younger man breaks down the barriers between employer and employee. The doctor's success in persuading Zirigu to talk about himself is significant: it implies that the African intellectual has a crucial role in ensuring that the voice of the unlettered folk may still be heard in a world that is increasingly inhospitable to them. Zirigu's story is representative enough. He was once a cook in the residence of the former white colonizers, but now he is performing the same service, with identical disadvantages, for their African successors.

Zirigu's story demonstrates that social inequities have continued in spite of independence. It also dramatizes how sexual roles were disrupted by colonialism, and how much this disruption has persisted after colonialism. As the doctor observes, Zirigu would not cook, in the context of his traditional culture, since that is a woman's job, but outside that culture, it was proper for him to cook for whites. As the doctor muses to himself, a black man is a man when his wife cooks for him, and he willingly occupies the woman's role when he cooks for whites. What then, the doctor wonders ironically, is a black man who cooks for other black men like the doctor himself (p. 17)?

The ironic question by the young doctor goes to the heart of Aidoo's theme. The confusions and the contradictions in sexual roles have cultural significance for they demonstrate that things have not changed in many respects in postcolonial society. The sense of permanence or continuity also has a positive side in this work by way of the stability and endurance which Aidoo usually attributes to her older Africans. Despite the injustices which still persist (he cannot obtain decent living conditions from the new government) Zirigu and his wife have managed to maintain their own dignity and sense of individual worth. He and Setu will never forget who they are, he asserts, even though he does have to ask his young employer to explain the meaning of the strange word, "independence" (p. 29).

Zirigu's request concludes the story on an appropriately ambiguous note. It combines his honesty and his naiveté, and these qualities are juxtaposed with the doctor's awareness of the real shortcomings of independence. The juxtaposition is one of innocent subversiveness (Zirigu's) and deliberate misgiving (the doctor's), and it reflects the degree to which Aidoo uses the growing intimacy between the two men to dramatize two distinct social views. The idealistic energies of the young generation is complemented by the gentleness and moral hardiness of the old. As a result, both men together reflect a kind of cultural duality in their world, one that is undergoing substantial as well as superficial changes. Once again Aidoo's handling of narrative perspective (two perspectives in this case) coincides perfectly with her theme.

In "No Sweetness Here" the perspective shifts to the insights of the Western-educated woman. The narrator is a school teacher through whose eyes we view Maami Ama, one of the women in the village. Maami is very attached to her son Kwesi—one of the narrator's students—but loses him, first to her estranged husband in a divorce, then to a fatal snake bite. The narrator's Western bearing takes the form of a certain sexual candor—evoking the image of sexually "liberated" women of Western, or Westernized, countries. She is therefore quite frank in admitting that she finds Kwesi's beauty attractive despite the fact that only an "immodest" woman like herself would comment on male beauty (pp. 56-57).

On the surface, Aidoo seems to be offering a simple contrast between a narrator whose education and occupation create the image of the self-sufficient outsider, and an older woman of traditional background. This apparent contrast is the more marked when we consider the emphasis on Maami's vulnerability. Her intense attachment to her son is as ambiguous as Mami Fanti's maternal fervor in "A Gift from Somewhere"—it both assures her claim to complete womanliness and compensates for her situation as a lonely mother in a society of capricious men like her husband Kodjo Fi. But Aidoo does not allow her readers to be sentimental about Maami's predicament. If Maami is the victim of Kodjo's selfish and bullying temper (p. 60), she is also victimized by her own weakness and by her lack of self-confidence. Quite clearly her society prizes and demands strength from its women as well as its men, the kind of strength which one senses beneath Mami Fanti's calculated innocence in "A Gift from Somewhere," in the hardiness of the old woman of "The Message," or the dogged survival of Zirigu and Setu in "For Whom Things Did not Change." By a similar token, the society is hard on those whose disposition places them in a position of inferiority or subordination.

Therefore, a bystander at the divorce proceedings declares that she hates women who cringe to males (p. 66). Maami herself acknowledges that the established customs allows her leverage in insisting on her rights in the matter of child custody, but for all that she loses Kwesi without a struggle. Without minimizing Maami's vulnerability as a woman or Kodjo Fi's culpability as a man, Maami lacks precisely those qualities which make Aidoo's rural women as attractive as they often are—a proud self-assurance and a resilience that is heightened rather than weakened by adversity. The attachment to Kwesi is not only a sign of her isolation, it is also a symptom of her insecurities and general weakness.

But looked at more closely, the contrast between a poised narrator and an insecure Maami is less clear-cut than it seems at first. If the mother's intense attachment to Kwesi compensates for her sense of isolation and vulnerability, so does the narrator's. Kwesi's future education, career, and even his sexual exploits have become a vicarious means of fulfillment for a woman whose education and occupation, albeit Western, have brought her a more limited degree of choice and mobility than her liberated language implies. Her absorption in Kwesi's future exposes the vulnerability and sense of limited opportunities which lie beneath the image of strength and assurance. It is also significant that this vicarious self-fulfillment through Kwesi excludes the domineering Kodjo Fi. Her reveries about Kwesi as the famous, much-traveled-man-of-the-world and lover always exclude his father (pp. 72-73). This is comparable with the manner in which a rural, uneducated woman like Mami Fanti excludes her husband from her dreams about her son in "A Gift from Somewhere."

The irony is that the progressive, liberated, and sophisticated image of the Western-educated woman is really a mask: underneath, there is the familiar vulnerability to the power of the male, and a new insecurity bred by the conflict between two cultural traditions. This is implied by the narrator's uneasy sense of kinship with the isolated and victimized mother of "No Sweetness Here." The title of the work has ironic implications for the work as a whole. On one hand, it rebuts the notion that the situation of rural women is all sweetness, a notion that has been fostered by the adventures of "bad" city women like Ekwensi's Jagua Nana who retreat to unspoilt rural roots to rediscover a lost innocence. On the other hand, the title offers an even more personal reference to the narrator's own individuality and to the lack of real "sweetness" and fulfillment behind her liberated Western image. After all, it is the educated Kwesis of the world who face a future of practically unlimited choices, not their female counterparts in rural classrooms.

Similarly, in "Everything Counts" the young university teacher who upholds her racial and sexual integrity by disdaining the national craze for European wigs still suffers from a sense of isolation, particularly since those Ghanaian "brothers" who have encouraged her militant African womanliness are still living comfortably, and indefinitely, in Europe as perpetual students with European girlfriends. The Western experience of the young intellectual brings with it a heightened awareness of the conflict between the sexes, for it appears that there are always disagreements over sexual images (wigs versus hair, for example) and choices. Finally, the cultural apostasy that seems inherent in the choice of European wigs is also intrinsic to the broader cultural choices of indiscriminately accepted Western values. How could she explain to her friends and relatives, the narrator muses, that they were hanging themselves with cars and refrigerators? (p. 6). The narrators of "No Sweetness Here" and "Everything Counts" command respect because they are acutely aware of the irony of their situation as supposedly liberated and independent Western women. The doubledealing of her "brothers" overseas and its implications for her own isolation are not lost on the narrator of "Everything Counts." The narrator's conscious identification with Maami and Kwesi in "No Sweetness Here" attest to her awareness that her own situation is no less vulnerable than Maami's, and that conversely, her advantage as an educated woman is not necessarily superior to that resiliency of spirit which marks the more effective, and illiterate, women whom Aidoo often discovers in the village.

There is no such awareness in the intensely satiric "Two Sisters," where Aidoo ironically dons the style of the woman's magazine format in order to take a close survey of the urban middle-class woman. Like "No Sweetness Here" and "Everything Counts," this story belongs to the third group of Aidoo stories in which the narrative viewpoint adopts the literate mode of standard English. Here the satiric emphasis leaves little room for sympathy with the Westernized Ghanaian woman. On one hand, there is Connie, unhappily married to a compulsive philanderer, and, on the other there is her sister Mercy whose notions of liberated womanhood take the form of a succession of affairs with married politicians, with their large cars and healthy bank accounts.

The plot is pointedly hackneyed, for the ultimate irony of the sisters' lives is the essentially deja vu quality of their borrowed middle-class aspirations. As Aidoo's personified Gulf of Guinea muses, people are worms whose lives are repetitions of old patterns (p. 96). In fact, this shift to the uninvolved point of view (the personified world of nature) heightens the more impersonal tone of this story, setting it apart from the personal, even private musings of the narrators in "Everything Counts" and "No Sweetness Here"—thereby effecting a greater sense of detachment from and hostility to the hand-me-down middle-class attitudes here. The sisters' tragedy as women, and the tragedy of their social milieu as a whole, consists of the fact that they are all living stereotypes whose experiences are a succession of secondhand clichés—Mercy's obsession with sexy clothes, uniformed chauffeurs, and vulgarly large American cars, and Connie's desperate determination to be respectably, even happily, married, and her hackneyed conviction that the new baby will somehow restore the marriage.

With her usual fastidious attention to thematic and technical details, Aidoo embellishes this description of a Westernized middle-class with all the popular banalities of women's magazines in the West. Unlike the acutely self-conscious narrator of "Everything Counts," the vapid Mercy thinks in clichés. As she prepares to leave the office at the end of the day's work, for example, she worries about the tediousness of taking a bus. It is just her luck, she complains to herself, that she does not have "one of those graduates for a boy-friend," someone who could come and fetch her home every evening. One man, Joe, is "dying" to take her home, but he only drives a taxi. Of course, he is "as handsome as anything," but. . . . (p. 87).

At the same time, Aidoo develops her satire by using standard English for fresh, original insights, just as readily as she deliberately uses hackneyed phrasing to expose limited personalities like Connie and Mercy. Connie's self-pitying tearfulness (her husband is late from work again) provides the occasion for a particularly telling ambiguity: he scorns the tears as the strongest weapons that a woman has in her "bitchy" arsenal (p. 96). The remark is effective in a very economical way. It succinctly exposes his callousness at the same time that it emphasizes the shallowness and the deliberate posturing to which women like Connie resort in their dealings with men.

As usual, Aidoo offers no pat answers or easy solutions here. Her insistence on portraying the woman's experience without transcendental resolutions remains a consistent strength of Aidoo's short fiction. We are left with the suggestively implausible resolutions at the end. Connie's baby effects a "magical" restoration of her failing marriage, a reconciliation that is suspect precisely because it is so sudden, so unfounded, and so obviously a mocking confirmation of Connie's wish fulfillment. As for Mercy, having barely survived one heart-breaking liaison she is all set to embark on another affair at the story's end, and her prospects are no more favorable than before. Like the ironic techniques of the narrative itself their lives have obviously settled into an unresolved repetition of old patterns.

This kind of deliberately inconclusive conclusion is further proof of Aidoo's frank realism, and of her refusal to treat her women on the basis of some idealistic wish fulfillment. The satire of Connie's hackneyed dreams amounts to a rejection of the popular literary clichés about an idealized womanhood. Consequently, the variety of viewpoints and the diverse situations which her stories bring together—from the strong old Esi Amfoa to the vapid young secretary—all emerge as distinct and existing facets of the woman's experience. The variety of styles and perspectives allows for a close awareness of the diversity of personalities with whom Aidoo is working. The close integration of each personal perspective with each narrative form creates an intimacy between protagonist and reader, and allows the reader to experience the central issue which links all of these diverse women. This is the sense of vulnerability and of limitations which inspires a proud self-assertiveness in the old women of "Certain Winds from the South" and "The Message," which encourages a covert subversiveness in "A Gift from Somewhere," or which explains that "bitchy" tearfulness which the male derides in "Two Sisters." Each woman's consciousness of her role as a woman enhances the compatibility of theme and form in Aidoo's short stories. Whether the individual's awareness is limited or admirably self-assured, the sense of established sexual patterns is formally—that is, structurally—reinforced by the manner in which the narrative as a whole becomes an extension of that individual's consciousness. On this basis, Aidoo's stories are neither haphazard devices nor lucky coincidences. They are carefully executed designs which blend with theme and character.

6

Flora Nwapa

While Aidoo's short stories are based on the skillful manipulation of diverse narrative forms, Flora Nwapa's technique as short-story writer is more uniform. This uniformity is not really a shortcoming in the work of this Nigerian writer. *This Is Lagos and Other Stories* actually owes much of its undeniable power to a consistently spare and taut style skillfully adapted to the writer's intense irony and to a brooding sense of tragedy throughout the collection.

The harsh social realism that pervades Nwapa's writings may very well be an effect of her own close involvement in public life in Nigeria. She received her early school education in eastern Nigeria where she also attended the University of Ibadan. After her graduation with a Bachelor of Arts degree, she received her Diploma in Education from Edinburgh University in 1958. Returning to Nigeria, she was appointed a Woman Education Officer, after which she taught high school for a number of years. Her public career has also included a term as assistant registrar at the University of Lagos, and more recently, a term as an elected official in the Nigerian government.

Nwapa's personal life has therefore involved a certain degree of public service that has inevitably exposed her to the workings of public institutions in contemporary Nigeria. This exposure is fairly evident in her short stories which are set in modern, urban Nigeria—particularly Lagos—and which deal with the lives of civil servants, teachers, and students, as well as the marginally educated immigrants from the rural areas. The uniform style of the collection arises from the fact that this world is invariably the setting of her stories—and from the additional fact that the main theme remains the same throughout. That theme centers on the lives of women in Nigeria's modern urban life, especially the traumas and disorientation to which these women are subjected. In Nwapa's short stories, Lagos and other cities are invariably destructive for seasoned city-dweller and rural newcomer alike.

The life style in Nwapa's cities is dominated by the continuous round of vicious sexual intrigues, domestic squabbles, tribal conflict, and civil war. That most familiar of city symbols, automobile traffic, sums up the confusions and conflicts of urban life. The ceaseless traffic jams of Lagos become living extensions of the individual disorientation and of the cultural disorder which the stories explore. The bloody mess of a typical traffic accident seems to be a fitting example of the psychic violence which the city holds out to women like Mama Eze who grew up in another world, in rural Nigeria. One day, while returning from work she witnesses such an accident, complete with the blood, the bodies, and the wrecked automobiles. When she forces herself to look more closely she even sees a severed human tongue on the ground.[1]

The description of the accident is terse, with a spareness of language that contrasts strikingly with the bloody horror of the subject matter. This kind of terseness underscores the pervasive sense of chaos and accumulating misfortunes in the lives of Nwapa's city women, and throughout her short stories. For example, in ''The Delinquent Adults'' a young man's death gradually escalates from the usual family misfortune into an intensely personal calamity for his helpless widow; and in ''Jide's Story'' the infidelities of a husband rapidly develop into a tragedy of abuse, with implications for his wife and for all women in his society. In stories like these the sense of tragedy, accentuated by the terse narrative style, is integrated with a carefully crafted impression of accelerating misfortune. The urban environment assumes the dimensions of some sinister destiny in the lives of Nwapa's characters.

The consistency and the relentlessness of Nwapa's narrative method encourage the suspicion that the human wastefulness and destructiveness that she describes are dreadfully continuous, even inexorable. In ''My Soldier Brother,'' for example, one son sets out for the battlefield (the story is set in war-time Biafra during the

Nigerian civil war)—immediately after the burial of his slain brother. His heroic bravado is counterbalanced by the grim realization that he is merely following his brother to the grave. The cruelty and the bloodiness that the war dramatizes only too well represent the sole continuity of any significance in their society. Death has become the overriding constant. Consequently the surviving brother no longer has any purpose in life except death—his enemies' and, inevitably, his own (*This is Lagos*, p. 117).

Conversely, the traditional joys of a homecoming are particularly intense in Nwapa's other short story on the war, "A Soldier Returns Home," not simply because of the usual values of family and local community, but because the humane continuities of family ties, communal traditions, even of life itself, have now been overshadowed by the tragic tribal conflicts that have sent the Ibo soldier in flight from western Nigeria to his eastern homeland, just before the outbreak of the civil war.

The references to the civil war are limited to these two stories, but the special dimensions of the war's violence (national and tribal conflict) are analogous to the social and personal turmoil that dominates the collection as a whole. The escalating tensions and conflicts in each story dramatize the increasing helplessness and vulnerability of women caught up in a world of tribal rivalries, social divisions, and the general dislocation of modern urban life. The title story of the collection ("This Is Lagos") is a fine example of the terse, understated manner in which the author gradually unfolds the perils of the city and the vulnerable situation of its women. Young Soha has come to live with her Lagos aunt (Mama Eze) with her mother's brief, pointed warning still ringing in her ears. It is said, the older woman observes, that the men in Lagos do not just chase the woman—they actually "snatch" them (p. 9).

The warning is actually the opening statement of the story, and it hangs ominously in the background throughout the first half of the narrative, ensuring an atmosphere of foreboding, even as we are told of Soha's sweet temper, her self-confidence, and her dutifulness. Indeed, it is indicative of Nwapa's considerable ability to evoke multiple responses to a uniform narrative style that the positive description of Soha's family and disposition is as disturbing as it is reassuring. Although the sentiments and images are positive reflections on Soha's personality and on her relatives, the clipped, noncommital language is a disturbing reminder of the tone and diction of her mother's earlier warning. For this reason, the narrative language maintains that initial sense of foreboding even in this apparently positive recital of close family ties and youthful innocence. Soha, we are reminded, is fond of her aunt, she is a "sweet girl," just twenty, "very pretty and charming," and "full of life." There is only one negative note in all of this, but offered in such a laconic manner that it almost escapes the reader. The sweet Soha shows a degree of confidence that is rare in a village girl just arrived in the big city, and she "pretended that she knew her mind" (p. 9). Soha's strengths turn out to be assumed (especially by the kindly, naive aunt) rather than real. The mother's initial warning has now been reinforced by that telltale sign of weakness, a kind of arrogance, in Soha herself ("She pretended that she knew her mind"). That warning assumes an increasingly urgent note as Mama Eze, and the reader, slowly realize that Soha has been secretly dating several men, that she has had to marry suddenly because of pregnancy, and that her estrangement from those prized family ties has become so complete that she and her husband have still failed, at the story's end, to pay the traditional visit of respect to her parents.

Throughout, the narrative viewpoint is centered on Mama Eze's perception. The accumulative design of the story—building from the opening warning to the complete breakdown of family ties and rural morality—is integrated with the gradual growth of Mama Eze's awareness. She gradually recognizes the changes in Soha's personality, and her bewilderment increases in direct proportion to the growing evidence of Soha's downfall. All of this exemplifies the finely controlled design of the Nwapa short story, one in which the simple, declarative opening (usually, as here, a warning or vaguely disturbing description) introduces a series of escalating conflicts or misfortunes. These misfortunes build up to an impending, or actual, catastrophe at the conclusion.

"The Road to Benin," set in Onitsha, also uses this accumulative design to convey an older generation's uneasiness with the unaccountable rebelliousness of educated urban youth. In "The Road to Benin" the older generation is also represented by a woman (Nwanyimma) who lives in the city but whose background is rural and nonliterate. Nwanyimma begins to lose her son in stages, beginning with his admission to high school. His new manners, typified by sullenness and rudeness, reflect the influences of a strange and violent world which is quite different from the ordered and generally familiar structures of his mother's rural past. Indeed, the boy's new behavior is puzzling to mother and reader alike precisely because no attempt is made to explain his actions or attitudes. They are, quite simply, the inexplicable and unexpected effects of his experiences in a world which has remained alien to Nwanyimma. The lack of explanation for his behavior is just as important as is its actual disruptiveness. It heightens the mysteriousness and destructiveness of his urban milieu, in Nwanyimma's eyes, and in turn it increases our awareness of Nwanyimma's limited experience and consequent vulnerability in that milieu.

Young Ezeka's growing delinquency eventually leads to a jail in Benin on charges of possessing the drug Indian hemp. This has also been a journey of sorts for Nwanyimma: her son's decline represents the progressive breakdown of the social and family traditions which have sustained her own identity and role as wife and mother. In keeping with Nwapa's finely discriminating sense of narrative irony, Nwanyimma's growing disorientation is actually emphasized by the sense of orderly progress which the narrative form suggests, particularly on the basis of that prevailing road symbol. When Nwanyimma literally takes to the Benin road in order to visit her son in jail, she returns not with composure, or with comforting knowledge, but with increased bewilderment, with the apprehension that there has been complete disintegration in her life. Even her familiar home looks strange to her when she returns from Benin. As usual, Nwapa terminates her story on this note of actual or impending disintegration, for the story ends with Nwanyimma still trying unsuccessfully to understand why her son is in jail, and why he would have slipped her some of the drug during her visit to the jail. She can only ask, pathetically, what did her son expect her to do with the drug? Neither her husband, to whom the question is addressed, nor anyone else in her world really has an answer for women like Nwanyimma. Their tragedy lies partly in the fact that unanswered questions like these are the very substance of their lives.

"The Traveller" also ends with an unanswered query, but here the question, asked by a young civil servant about an acquaintance, is really rhetorical. She is wondering what kind of woman her male friend thinks she is (p. 8). The woman, Bisi, has been educated in a British university, has lived and worked in Lagos for most of her adult life, and unlike older women like Mama Eze and Nwanyimma is quite familiar with the ways of the city, its traffic, its perpetual confusion, and its scheming men. Mr. Busa, the "traveller" of the story, has called on Bisi several times during a visit to Lagos—the story actually begins, in Nwapa's typically arresting opening, with his knock on her apartment door. At each meeting Mr. Busa tries to take Bisi to bed, but is rebuffed by her tactics of polite evasion and passive resistance. Bisi's tactics contribute to that dramatic suspense which Nwapa often derives from the accumulative effects of her narrative design. This suspense is heightened by the fact that Bisi's subtle rebuffs not only discomfit Mr. Busa, they also make her own motives uncertain to the reader. She becomes ambiguous and the reader is unsure, almost to the very end, about the outcome of this running contest with the persistent Mr. Busa.

For this actually is a contest. Mr. Busa's male arrogance leads to a self-defeating and clumsy directness that is increasingly unable to counter Bisi's durable self-protectiveness. On her side, Bisi masks her hostility and her craftiness with an engaging openness and a seeming vulnerability. In retrospect there is a telling irony in the opening image of the story— Bisi readily opening her room door to Mr. Busa's initial knock. It creates a misleading impression that Bisi is easily accessible, stirring the reader's uneasiness just as effectively as it arouses Mr. Busa's futile expectancy. Moreover, the tensions of this contest are heightened by the laconic tone of Bisi's style and Nwapa's narrative as a whole:

He came closer and kissed her. But she did not return the kiss. She switched on the engine, and was about to drive off when he said, urgently, "Wait. . . .

"You don't seem to believe me. What I have been doing has been the accumulation of my feelings for you for a long time, even at College."

"Really?" (p. 7).

The casual narrative style complements Bisi's own personality and it blends, pointedly, with her own style. This casualness has the striking effect of making her appear weak and vulnerable, but this impression of weakness and uncertainty is deceptive. Bisi knows very well what she is doing. When she asks her friend Sophia that question which concludes the story the following morning, she knows the answer. She knows what kind of woman a man like Mr. Busa thinks she is. Her question is a rhetorical statement that vents her scorn of Mr. Busa and his kind. It expresses her indignation at male selfishness and insensitivity towards women, attitudes that also typify her middle-class, civil servant world as well as the urban experience. On this basis, her question brings to a climactic conclusion the gradual unmasking or revelation which is effected by the evolving drama of her contest with Mr. Busa. The tantalizing and sometimes disturbing ambiguities have given way to an unequivocal statement of her position.

Notwithstanding the conclusiveness of Bisi's triumph, the very arrogance of Mr. Busa's tactics and the very vigor with which Bisi must protect her integrity (and the issue for her is integrity, not chastity per se) tend to underscore the shakiness of the woman's situation in Bisi's urban milieu. Women like her enjoy a worldly self-confidence which is the result of their education, independence as job holders, and general experience in the ways of the city. This is the basis on which Bisi is contrasted in another story ("The Child Thief") with a woman who lacks her education, as well as her independence, as a single, employed woman. At the same time, the Bisis of Lagos are also susceptible to male exploitiveness, partly because of personal limitations and partly because of external pressures—the pressures of sexual intrigues, middle-class social climbing (in which men hold out tempting ladders to ambitious young women), and the exciting uprootedness of urban life. Indeed, the central paradox of their lives, one that lends itself to a certain irony, is the fact that the education, the socioeconomic independence, and the social "liberation" of these women can be perilous as well as protective. The advantages of their world can be real strengths to someone like Bisi who enjoys a certain toughmindedness and secure knowledge of self. For others with an itch to be superficially sophisticated, the trappings of Western education and jobs merely accentuate the deeply rooted insecurities and dependency which make them vulnerable. In the case of the latter, the standard English and Western format of Nwapa's short story emphasizes this borrowed sophistication.

Amedi ("The Loss of Eze") is one of these brittle sophisticates. She, too, is a civil servant with all of Bisi's advantages and social independence. However, under her professional success and general savoir faire Amedi suffers from a potentially self-destructive dependency on men. The loss of her boyfriend Eze, to another woman, has left her severely despondent and temporarily without self-confidence. The terse Nwapa style evokes Amedi's despairing sense of loss in the typically arresting statement of the opening paragraphs: "I thought my heart would break when I lost Eze. . . . " (p. 81). Conversely, her return to life, at the embassy party that is the setting for the story, has really been assured by her meeting with another man, Tunde. She discovers that Tunde is the nicest person she has ever met—a discovery that is identical to her first impressions of the now "lost" Eze (p. 92).

Amedi's return to life actually confirms her continuing dependency on men for her most fundamental feelings of fulfillment and self-worth. On the basis of the story, she has failed to learn any substantial lessons from her experience; there is no evidence that she has acquired any new capacity for emotional independence or, most importantly, self-protectiveness. Those echoes of the earlier meeting with Eze—the nicest person she had ever met—conclude the story on a note of foreboding. There is a clear suggestion here that the new relationship with Tunde, another "nicest" person, will simply repeat the old self-destructive cycle.

In "Jide's Story" limitations of this sort result in a major tragedy for the women. As a university student in London Jide Ogun marries another Nigerian, Rose, whom he leaves in London upon his return home to enter the civil service. He meets and has a series of affairs with a number of women, including Maria, and he continues his infidelities quite openly even after Rose has returned from London. Maria becomes unusually possessive, even claiming, to his consternation, that he is her husband and the father of her two children. He eventually learns that her bizarre claim results from the fact that she is insane, and that her insanity has been the effect of an extremely unhappy marriage to a cruel man while she was a student in London. Meanwhile, Jide is increasingly puzzled by his wife. Rose never reproaches him for his affairs, she never questions his actions, and while she scrupulously fills the usual role of wife and homemaker, it is clear that she has withdrawn completely from her husband into a silence which mystifies him but which is really her mode of revenge and self-protection.

Of the seven stories dealing with the experiences of women, this is the only one in the collection which is written from the man's point of view. This tactic is particularly effective: Rose's revenge of silence and withdrawal is the more striking precisely because it is presented from the mystified viewpoint of the guilt-ridden Jide. Indeed, her silence envelops her with a mysterious aura that owes much of its awesomeness to the distance from which Jide is forced to view her. In turn, that distance and mystery enhance the self-protectiveness with which Rose responds to that predatory, often insensitive, maleness which has already destroyed Maria, and now threatens Rose herself. Rose's conjugal silence serves the same defensive functions as the loud Bohemian manners of the single young women who are Jide's neighbors. Finally, the male's moral responsibility in the tragedy of women like Maria and Rose is underscored by the reader's intimacy with the male's viewpoint, and with the guilt that is gradually exposed through the typically accumulative effects of Nwapa's short-story form. Accordingly, the development of the plot is skillfully protracted by playing upon Jide's curiosity, and the reader's, about Rose's reactions to the events around her. It is the man whose story ends with a demoralizing question without answers, the kind of question which illuminates the woman's vulnerability as well as strength by emphasizing the man's confusion and insecurities (Does Rose herself realize that there is a barrier between them? Or has she too been cheating on their marriage?). The fact that this kind of disturbing question is being asked by the male provides another impressive example of Nwapa's ability to vary the effect, or use, of a consistent narrative technique (in this case, the conclusion of a story with demoralizing statements or open-ended questions).

The pressures and the cruelty which force Rose into withdrawal and bring Maria to insanity are the dominant themes of "The Child Thief," a story in which the gradual accumulation of narrative details dramatize a woman's slow descent into madness. The woman is Agnes, a former schoolmate of the free-spirited Bisi, now an unhappy and childless wife whose husband neglects her in favor of a woman who has borne him children. The contrasts between Bisi and Agnes, upon which Bisi herself reflects, stress the special handicaps of women like Agnes. She has had only a limited education which uproots her from traditional social roles without being able to confer social or economic independence; her marriage makes her more susceptible to the male's power and privileges as they exist both in the older and modern areas of Nigerian life; and that susceptibility is increased by the childlessness which is a disaster for traditional and modern women alike. Agnes suffers all of the major disadvantages of women in both the old and new societies, and she represents a rather pointed contrast with Bisi whose independence springs not only from her education, job, and social position, but, significantly, from her personal strengths (a no-nonsense concern for her freedom and integrity) and from her status as a single woman. On the other hand, Agnes remains fat, untidy and self-pitying as she slips gradually into the madness which leads her to the hospital nursery where she steals the baby that she cannot conceive.

She is promptly detected, and the story ends with her arrest and with the ignominy of a husband who must follow her to the police station as curious neighbors look on. There is no compensatory note of self-protective strength here. The story's conclusion does not even offer the consoling reminder of Bisi's contrasting resiliency, for Bisi drops out of the narrative once she has served to introduce Agnes and the latter's plight to the reader. Instead, what we are left with is the discomfiting sensation, enforced by that relentlessly accumulative format, that Agnes' situation has been progressively degenerating and that it is now completely out of control and beyond rational direction. Her life has been a depressing one-way slide into an unrelieved wretchedness—from the short-lived happiness of the early days of marriage to loneliness and feelings of inadequacy as a childless woman, and, at the end, the total disintegration of both Agnes and her home. There is a precise narrative logic in this sequence of events, with each cause leading inexorably to its inevitable effect. In the process, the narrative order or form becomes an ironic mode, because its logical coherence emphasizes the confusions and disorder which it enables us to discover in Agnes's experience. At this point, Nwapa's rather fastidious sense of narrative order and uniformity enhances that ironic insight which informs her short story as tragedy.

Only "The Delinquent Adults" really equals the achievement of "The Child Thief" in what is generally an impressive collection of stories. Agnes' misfortunes arise equally from her own inadequacies and from the external pressures on childless wives and semi-educated women. In "The Delinquent Adults" Ozoemena's troubles result both from her new status as a widow and from her own lack of initiative and self-confidence. This is a finely crafted work, a striking example of Nwapa's penchant for gradually developing dramatic tension and structure in her narratives. The story opens on a forbidding, vaguely threatening note: Ozoemena has just been dreaming that her husband crossed a strange river, leaving her and their two children behind. The dream is a foreboding of her husband's death and, from this point, Ozoemena's fortunes deteriorate rapidly. Her husband is killed in a traffic accident, in fulfillment of the dream's prophecy. The familiar symbolism of the automobile and city traffic prepares us for the dislocation and violent psychic upheaval which the accident introduces to Ozoemena for the first time in her life. After the funeral she returns to their rural home outside the city (Port Harcourt), only to discover that her husband's relatives hate and suspect her of the worst things. They insinuate that she was responsible for her husband's death by virtue of her dream, and, refusing to believe that she has turned over all of her husband's belongings, they are now planning to force her to give up his "bags" of money. At the conclusion of the story she is faced with the seemingly impossible task of supporting herself and her children without resources (because of her limited education she cannot find a good job) and without even minimal help from her family.

Her difficulties are further compounded by the lack of initiative that stems from the dependency of a woman who had long ago invested her future in the role of a wife, and who had subordinated her own talents to the needs of a marriage. In this regard, she is the classical example of the woman who chooses to live in both worlds at the same time, foregoing the education which alone could guarantee personal security of sorts—in order to choose married life in an urban environment which demands self-sufficiency rather than total dependency (or traditional rural family roles) of its women. Ozoemena is really incapable of making decisions about her future. Her paralysis emerges at the end of the story as a damning reflection of the built-in handicaps of the kind of female role and upbringing which she had freely chosen. The fact that she chose this role—abandoning school for marriage against the advice of friends and teachers—underscores Ozoemena's own responsibility for her present predicament. For, like Aidoo, Nwapa does not allow her women the comparatively easy role of innocent victims and martyrs of social injustice. The patterns of social injustice are real enough, and in Ozoemena's case they are palpable in the domineering and insolent bearing of her brother-in-law, or in the repulsive older man who tries to bribe her into his bed with vague promises of support for her children and herself. But in the final analysis Ozoemena and Nwapa's other urban women bear a substantial measure of responsibility for their own fates, particularly since their urban, literate world offers them options which, if taken, can partly compensate for the prevailing disadvantages of being a woman in a violent and exploitive society. Female emancipation is both external (the liberalization of social institutions and traditions) and internal (the ideal development of the woman's personal strength and initiative), and Ozoemena's tragedy springs from the failure of both forms of emancipation in her own life.

Ozoemena's difficulties are further compounded by the fact that she lacks the kind of family support which the old rural traditions once offered the bereaved in times of need. Instead, she becomes a victim of the manner in which family traditions have been corroded by recent history. Her own mother has no assistance to offer except that abortive and humiliating "arrangement" with the wealthy old man, and her husband's family continues to abuse her, despising her as an untrustworthy city outsider. As a final irony, the story which opens with her dream-prophecy of her husband's death now closes with unmistakable signs that she herself may be in danger. The husband's family has consulted a dibia (a priest) about those vexing bags of money, they are convinced that she is lying, and there is no telling how far they will go the next day when they will compel Ozoemena to swear the truth "by the gods." The collapse of Ozoemena's world now represents the general decay of social institutions and moral values around her—including the time-honored traditions of family ties. The premonition of more trouble for Ozoemena *beyond* the story's conclusion presages the further decline of those institutions and values. The narrative momentum that flows directly from Nwapa's accumulative structure and which enables us to anticipate events after the ending of the story has therefore become a formal or aesthetic symbol, representing the continuity, or momentum, of social events and values in a process of steady decline.

On the whole it appears that Nwapa's very choice of genre, as well as her choice of techniques within the selected genre, are interwoven with her most fundamental perspectives. Her perception of contemporary life in urban Nigeria demands a short-story format, one that does not depend to any significant degree on the kind of oral modes that are so integral to much of Aidoo's short fiction. It is a format which reflects the largely literate, Western middle-class world within which her women move (as in the case of Bisi or Amedi). That literate world's dominance in the lives of older, rural-oriented women like Mama Eze is emphasized by the uniformly literate method which describes *their* experiences. In Nwapa's hands the short story seems especially appropriate for brief, even deliberately unfinished glimpses of urban life. Thus many of the stories leave their protagonists in the middle of seemingly insoluble crises, or at best, in the face of disturbing and unanswerable questions. Taken together, these suggestively abbreviated vignettes suggest the fragmentary nature of the social experiences out of which they arise. In addition, the spare language which Nwapa sustains throughout suggests that thinness of spirit and that limited humaneness which the stories themselves attribute to the society as a whole.

The rural and largely traditional world of the older Nigeria, as it is envisaged by Nwapa, seems to require a different style—an expansive use of language reflecting the formal richness and ornate modes of traditional oral cultures. It seems to demand the detailed duplication of those social conventions intrinsic to everyday relationships in that milieu of elaborately defined roles. When Nwapa turns to that milieu she selects the genre that most easily accommodates an expansive language and elaborate design, for these features reflect the complexities of a society that is always more ambiguous (fulfilling in some respects, while limiting in others) than the general meagerness of urban life. She selects the novel.

The Nwapa novel is typical of the kind of African novel that resists purely Western-oriented approaches to the genre. It has been a truism for some time now that the African novel is a Western import, differing from the drama and the short story in that the latter have partly developed from ritual folk drama and the oral tale respectively. There are inherent problems, however, in approaching the African novel as if it were a wholly foreign import, problems that arise from using criteria which follow the theory, practice, and criticism of the novel in the West. These problems do not always materialize, for it is not difficult to find African novelists who pattern their themes and narrative forms on their own experience of Western individualism and art—either in the West or in their own countries.

Matters are not quite so simple in the case of other African writers. The issue of social realism, for example, has long been de rigeur in the study of the novel in the West, but critics who are sensitive to cultural differences know how relative the very notion of realism can be as they follow the novel from the West to Africa. What may be socially unrealistic or romantic for the Western reader is not necessarily so for the Yoruba reader of Amos Tutuola's fiction. Similarly, the issues of individualism that so often dominate Western society and literature are not always as crucial in novels by some Africans. The cultural distinctions that are involved here were summed up in 1938 by a young anthropologist, Jomo Kenyatta:

If it is true that the European system of education aims at individuality, is it then to be wondered at that Europeans educated in this way have some difficulty in finding the right place for the organic tribal relationships of the Africans? We may sum it up by saying that to the Europeans "Individuality is the ideal of life," to the Africans the ideal is the right relations with, and behaviour to, other people. No doubt educational philosophy can make a higher synthesis in which these two great truths are one, but the fact remains that while the Europeans place the emphasis on one side the Africans place it on the other.[2]

The question which Kenyatta both raises and answers has immediate significance for the study of the novel in Africa. Given those organic tribal relationships which he notes, how useful is it to discuss those African novels which describe traditional, or non-Westernized African societies, by applying to such novels those criteria of individualism which are so sacrosanct in Western society and literature? This is the kind of question that is being raised by a few critics in the West itself, among them the American James Olney who (in noting Kenyatta's remarks) has emphasized what has always been obvious but not always conceded by Western students of non-Western fiction: "No doubt the Western literary critic who picks up an African novel will unconsciously be carrying in his overnight bag all the philosophical and psychological assumptions programmed into him as he grew up, as he pursued his studies in the Western tradition, as he read the masterpieces of Western literature." The European or American reader for whom individualism is an ideal "cannot hope to read, with full comprehension or imaginative sympathy," the writings of those Africans for whom social relations and the social organism are the paramount ideals.[3]

Kenyatta's caveat and Olney's rider apply to the study of those aspects of African literature which originate with, and describe, indigenous cultural traditions or the interaction between those traditions and non-African civilizations—the plays of Soyinka and Sutherland, for example, much of Chinua Achebe's fiction and all of Tutuola's novels. Flora Nwapa's novels deserve special attention because they have been the most neglected yet the most striking examples of African novel-writing manifestly motivated and shaped by a communal rather than predominantly individualistic perspective. More specifically, the Nwapa novel is not so much a study of the individual as it is a reenactment of the relationship between individual and community. Her titles, *Efuru* and *Idu*, are likely to mislead those Western readers whose literary experience (by way of "name" titles like *Jane Eyre*, *Madame Bovary*, and *Ulysses*) may encourage the expectation that Nwapa, like her European predecessors, concentrates primarily on the individual's private perceptions.[4] Although she retains and demonstrates her distinctive individuality and personal needs, the Nwapa heroine is also crucial as the main focus of her community's attention and as the symbolic hub of those relationships and behavioral patterns which Kenyatta emphasizes.

The community's collective perception of Efuru, or of Idu, is as crucial in the novel's theme and structure as her reaction to the community and its traditions. Nwapa's "name" title therefore identifies the focal point of the community's attention as much as it pinpoints the individual's personal experience within the community. The community's attention and its relationship with the Nwapa protagonist are defined and communicated by a dialogue format which bears all the signs of the novelist's careful attention to oral forms that reinforce her communal themes. To read the Nwapa novel is to be immersed to a remarkable degree in a ceaseless flow of talk. Her fictive structure relies on the barest minimum of indirect commentary, and depends instead on a continuous series of dialogues, all designed to dramatize the main concerns of the novel. In a general sense, the decided orality of Nwapa's fiction is compatible with the communal experience which her work shares with novelists like Tutuola, but the sheer volume of talk in *Efuru* and *Idu* is Nwapa's distinguishing hallmark, and so are the frankly sociosexual themes which dominate this oral, or auditory, experience. Talk, more specifically the talk of women, establishes the milieu within which Nwapa examines the community's expectations of its women as well as the woman's response to both the community and her own needs.

Nwapa leaves no doubt about the extent to which this oral format has been consciously incorporated within her themes and narrative design. In a work like *Idu*, for example, the speakers are very conscious of talk itself as both experience and a mode of judgement: talking is the art of social discourse and it is a process of reliving experiences in order to evaluate them. Sometimes, after she has discussed anything she returns to it and talks it over again, confides Uzoechi, one of Nwapa's inveterate talkers (p. 29). Uzoechi's personal view of talk clearly corresponds with the significance of conversation and dialogue in Nwapa's fiction as a whole. Talk influences personal attitudes and social relationships by reenacting pertinent experiences. Even without this power of reenactment, talk may determine judgement by offering clues to the speaker's moral character. In *Idu*, a woman who talks too much is not usually taken seriously, and her reputation as the bringer of bad news is generally in keeping with her disagreeable disposition. On the other hand, talk can be just as significant by virtue of its absence; knowing when to be silent is a highly prized sign of prudence or sensitivity. Even the loquacious Nwasobi counsels silence regarding the illness of Adiewere (Idu's husband) lest malicious enemies take advantage of his illness; Idu does not wish to mortify her childless friend by telling her about her own pregnancy; and everyone refrains from discussing the village's worst kept secret (one of the men's sterility) partly out of solicitude and partly out of a sense of bowing to divine will.

If talking or silence is a form of analysis or judgement, then listening, or failing to hear, is an indication of one's involvement in, or separation from, the community's experience. In *Idu*, the recurring dialogues between Nwasobi and her friend Uzoechi reflect the unflagging zeal with which they make everybody's business the community's business, and each is not above chiding the other for having failed to hear any piece of news which they might now be discussing. Uzoechi will therefore taunt Nwasobi, apropos of the news of Idu's long-awaited pregnancy. She is amazed that the latter has not heard the news while she who only returned home the day before knows all that has happened (pp. 42-43). Talk, intimate and prolonged talk, is the hallmark of personal closeness between perpetual gossips like Nwasobi and Uzoechi, or between special friends like Idu and Ojiugo who can talk far into the night about trade, husbands, and about all of the local topics (p. 37). In a more general sense, the pervasive patterns of talk in Nwapa's fiction are also a symptom of the oral basis of the village's communal structure —ranging from the shouts of "Ewuu" that announce a suicide, to the imprecations with which an unknown thief is denounced by the victim to the village at large.

Altogether, both as a mode of judgement and as a reflection of the communal structure, the ability to converse, or to remain silent, indicates a certain sense of order and propriety both in social relationships and in the individual's role in those relationships. Consequently Nwapa's dialogues are dominated throughout by a strong sense of proper form. Note, for example, how carefully an exchange between Idu and her old friend Nwasobi is constructed with an eye, and ear, to the propriety of statement and correctness of judgement. As usual, Nwasobi is straining to bring up the latest news (in this instance, Idu's rumored pregnancy) without being rude and abrupt, while Idu's circumlocutory style only heightens the drama of it all by prolonging Nwasobi's suspense, and in the midst of all this, Idu lectures her sister Anamadi on hygiene. Dramatic suspense has been skillfully blended with the careful formality of dialogue and with the proper forms of social intercourse and personal health:

"Is market good these days for you?" asked Nwasobi.
"It is bad."
"That's what every trader says."
"It is not a lie. The market is bad. But we have to go on trading as there is nothing else we can do. The season will soon be over. I want to rest when the season is over. I don't feel very well these days."
"Is it true?" The older woman caught on to this before they went on to other topics.
"Yes, I have not been well for some time. I even went to Iyienu hospital."
. . . "Anamadi, come and take the plate away," she said to her young sister, "and give me water to wash my hands, and some drinking water too."
Anamadi fetched some water in a basin and when Idu was finished washing her hands she stood there waiting.
"You want me to ask you again after washing my hands, to bring me drinking water. This girl, what can we do with her?" asked Idu in despair (pp. 45-46).

In a more somber vein this circumlocutory structure and the formal sense of order which it imposes on the dialogue heighten the suspense and air of propriety in an otherwise commonplace exchange between Idu and Amarajeme, for she now knows that his wife Ojiugo has deserted him because of his sterility, and on his side he is wondering whether she knows this:

"Welcome, Idu, have you come to see me today? Is all well that you have come?"
"Our Amarajeme, I said I must come for I have not seen you for a long time. Last night I asked about you, you were in the Great River."
"Yes, I went to my second home. You know that one is always longing for the place where one was brought up."
"It is true. Were they all well when you left them?"

"It was a long time ago. My father-in-law and mother-in-law were well when I left them."

"Your father-in-law and mother-in-law?"

"Yes, didn't you know that I was married before I married your friend?"

"Is it true?"

"You know, Idu, you know."

"Truly I didn't know."

"Your friend didn't tell you?"

"She didn't tell me. What happened to your first wife?"

"She died before my manhood could be tested."

Idu stoped. She did not say anything. She wondered whether somebody had broken the news to him. . . .

"You are quiet," observed Amarajeme. "Why? How is market?"

"Market is going on well" (pp. 130-31).

These dialogues are fairly representative of Nwapa's skills in developing oral forms into effective narrative devices. They suggest a careful attention, on the novelist's part, to dramatic development and suspense, to a sense of moral and social order, and to a sense of design in both society and her art. They are also the means of integrating the social and moral significance of talk in the community with the novel's structure as a whole: the scrupulously developed sense of design in each dialogue is really a part of the larger design of the novel's total structure. At the same time, the formal or moral order, represented by the dialogue and by the narrative structure as a whole, symbolizes the social relationships and individual experience that her themes describe. The community's perception of the woman's personality and the woman's response to the community are all presented through oral experiences (especially dialogue and storytelling) and in turn those oral experiences reflect "relations with, and behaviour to, other people."

The oral techniques of *Efuru*, the first novel, are based in part on the dialogue structure which is much more fully developed in *Idu*. In *Efuru* these techniques also reflect Nwapa's indebtedness to oral literature. The analytical commentary that is familiar in the Western novel is often replaced by the narrative formula of oral storytelling, particularly in narrative commentary which is based on general time references rather than specific dates, on elliptical rather than precise narrative detail, and on the archetypal rather than personal identity of some characters:

One day, Efuru and Ogea came to see Nnona in the hospital. They brought her live oguna fish. . . . Any time Nnona's granddaughter wanted to cook for her grandmother, she would take two oguna fish, kill them and use them in cooking.

One day the girl went to the stream and, when she came back, she saw that the pot of soup she had cooked for her grandmother was gone. Somebody had come while she was away and took the pot of soup. She sat down and wept (p. 161).

In evoking the style of oral literature, the novelist incorporates into her own narrative those indigenous traditions which the style represents. The theft of a pot of soup is not simply a crime, in the strictly legalistic sense, against Nnona and her granddaughter. It is also an act of sacrilege against the community and against the moral order, and it is eventually punished by the diety Uhamiri (the Woman of the Lake) when the thief's hand is bitten by the stolen fish. The oral style evokes the established values of communal life and the traditional moral order represented by the old deities. In a similar vein, the traditional word games and play songs of children represent those ideals of family unity, house building, and social roles (especially the roles of mothers) which are important in Efuru's society. The recital of a folk tale becomes a symbolic ritual within Nwapa's larger narrative. In this case, the story describes the successful effort of Nkwo to rescue her sister from the clutches of an evil spirit after the other sisters (Eke, Orie, and Afo) had refused their help. The conquest and destruction of the spirit affirm the communal and family ties which Nkwo defends. This social continuity is linked with the continuity of life itself: the protagonist's predicament and eventual triumph are played out against a very specific time background, for her sisters' names are also the names of the days of the week.

The communal traditions which Nwapa's oral techniques evoke are crucial to Efuru's experience in the novel. Efuru is a beautiful woman who is admired by the community for her business acumen as a trader, for her integrity and generosity, as well as for her beauty. Despite her admirable qualities, she cannot seem to sustain satisfactory relationships with men. After two unsuccessful marriages she finally determines that her personal fulfillment has to be attained, not by the conventional female roles of wife and mother, but by being alone and independent. She therefore chooses to

dedicate herself as special worshipper of Uhamiri, the Woman of
the Lake, the deity whose childlessness and role (the giver of beauty
and wealth to women) correspond with Efuru's desire to be alone
and independent. Efuru's marriages fail, in part, because the conventional selfishness of men within the traditional marriage structure is incompatible with her sense of self. Her integrity as an
individual is violated by her husbands' casual assumption that she
will be the long-suffering, perpetually forgiving, and deferent
figure upon which many women have customarily modeled their
roles as wives. Consequently the Woman of the Lake is really Efuru's
alter ego, a being who symbolizes her independent spirit, her superior talents as a businesswoman, and her general capacity for
self-fulfillment.

Efuru's story is essentially one of growth. First, she develops
from an early innocence, based on a general acceptance of conventional definitions of woman as wife and mother, into an ambiguous phase in which she tries to be the conventional wife while,
at the same time, demonstrating a healthy disregard for norms that
seem irrelevant or unduly restrictive. Then, in a later stage of
growth, she becomes more deliberately detached from the role of
wife and more drawn into another role (the worshipper of Uhamiri),
one that is admittedly sanctioned by the community's traditions
but which is also more compatible with her individual needs rather
than with the community's pervasive expectations of women as
wives and mothers. Her growth is marked by changes in her relationship with the traditions of her society. If the echoes of the oral
tales emphasize the general sense of established conventions throughout the narrative, then it is the dialogue structure, already well
developed in this first novel, which enables Nwapa to subject Efuru's
personality and growth to the communal judgements and value
systems that are inherent in the oral mode. When she flouts convention by going to live with Adizua (her first husband) without a
formal betrothal and without the payment of the bride price, the community—the collective guardian of those conventions—makes its
voice heard, first in the dialogue between those farmers who are
peeved by this kind of indifference to ancestral customs, then in
the exchanges between market-women who are astounded at the
inequality, and unconventionality, of the match (pp. 7, 16).

As narrative commentary on Efuru's actions and experience, the dialogues are fairly varied. They reflect a cross-section of communal opinions, and they represent the diverse personalities of the speakers who are sometimes identified only by group (friends, market-women, farmers, or relatives)—thereby enhancing their archetypal and communal significance—and who really function as a ubiquitous chorus with inevitable opinions on every detail of Efuru's life. Accordingly, neighbors gossip, as they invariably do when Efuru remains childless after a year of marriage. From their point of view, she is not a real woman: she is barren (p. 23). When this "problem" recurs during Efuru's second marriage (to Eneberi) the comments are essentially the same. In this case the commentators are identified (Eneberi's mother and a friend). Their settled views of women, marriage, and motherhood are appropriately conveyed in highly formal dialogue reflecting a strong sense of social and rhetorical order and moving slowly from formal preliminaries to circumlocution, thence to a direct discussion of the immediate topic. The highly formal structure of the dialogue reinforces the conservative viewpoint of the speakers:

"Oh, is that you, Omirima? Welcome Nwadugwu," Gilbert's [Eneberi's] mother greeted her visitor.
"Our Amede, Nwezebuona. How are you?" the woman asked.
"We are well. You have come to see us today?"
"Yes, I have come to see you today."
"Is it well?"
"It is very well. I just said I should call on you today. It is very well."
Gilbert's mother called someone who brought kola.
"I took some purgative medicine. I won't take kola."
"Ew-o-o is that so? All right you can take the kola home, it is yours." . . .
"Amede, I am going, I just said I should come and greet you today. Where is your son's wife? Has she gone to the market or somewhere?"
"She has gone to the stream with her husband. . . . "
"And has she told you anything yet?" the woman continued.
"No, she has not told me anything yet. But did you hear anything?"
"No, I have not heard anything, that's why I have come to you. It is a year since your son married. One year is enough for any woman who would have a baby to begin making one. Find out quickly and if she is barren start early to look for a black goat" (pp. 173-74).

The dialogue form not only communicates the community's collective opinions about Efuru, it also has an important narrative function, helping to mark those narrative stages through which Efuru grows into a mature and self-sufficient womanhood. This narrative structure is best exemplified by the manner in which the Woman of the Lake is gradually introduced, by stages, into the narrative, beginning with a series of casual references to the deity (when she punishes the fish-thief, for example) and culminating with several detailed discussions about her significance in Efuru's life. These later discussions (including Efuru's description of her recurrent dreams of the goddess) coincide with Efuru's growing restiveness in her traditional role as wife. The recurring nature of the dream actually duplicates the repetitive allusions to the goddess in the narrative. In turn, Efuru's father finally establishes the explicit connections between Efuru and the deity when he explains his daughter's dream—Uhamiri has chosen Efuru as a special worshipper (p. 183).

The gradual clarification of the links between Efuru and Uhamiri corresponds with the direction and gradual development of Efuru's growth. Uhamiri's symbolic presence also clarifies the precise significance of that growth within the crucial context of communal traditions, for that presence is an assurance that in developing into a more self-sufficient and independent woman, Efuru is not growing into the kind of self-contained individualism which would break away from the cultural and religious heritage represented by Uhamiri herself. Efuru achieves independence within the community, not outside it, and her individualism is sanctioned by one set of the community's traditions (enshrined by the deity's presence) despite the fact that it departs from another set of traditions (centered on the woman's more conventional roles as wife and mother). As a further indication of how carefully Nwapa has integrated the woman's growth and identity with the narrative structure as a whole, it is possible to trace Efuru's development on a variety of levels that are distinct but very closely related. First, Efuru's earlier development is largely predicated upon the preparation of a young woman for the usual roles of mother and wife, and it is marked by a series of formal rites and conventions that are appropriate to such roles. Secondly, even as she takes part in these conventional rituals, Efuru displays that individualism which will eventually lead to her rejection of marriage and motherhood, and as a consequence, her education in the conventions of traditional womanhood is essentially ambiguous. Even as it prepares her for the traditional roles it also becomes part of the overall growth which eventually culminates in her religiously sanctioned declaration of independence. Thirdly, the ambiguity of this education (conventional in design and purpose, but anticonventional in effect) corresponds with the diverse, even contradictory, friendships cultivated by Efuru, from the conventionally long-suffering, self-effacing Ossai (her first mother-in-law) to the sturdily independent neighbor, Ajanupu. Finally, Efuru's social growth, into a traditional role then into independence, is linked with a cosmic issue. The novel as a whole envisions growth itself as part of the continuing, universal changes which are dictated by time (the cycle of birth, life, and death) and which are implicit in those rituals and conventions (relating to puberty, marriage, and parenthood), through which men and women are prepared for their sexual roles in society.

Efuru meets her first husband, Adizua, after that festival in which young people are supposed to select their sexual partners (p. 1). This reference to the festival initiates a series of ceremonies and conventions through which the young Efuru, and others like her, prepare for the customary duties of womanhood. The rite of circumcision (clitoridectomy) and the custom of fattening the prospective bride are followed by the payment of the dowry and the formalization of the marriage to Adizua. Efuru's failure to have a child after a year of marriage results in the mandatory fertility ceremonies which a dibia (holy man) prescribes and which are intended to guarantee a pregnancy. When she does become pregnant she undergoes the necessary rituals which ensure her own health and the future well-being of the child. The birth itself is followed by prescribed postnatal ceremonies to facilitate the long life of the baby girl Ogonim. After Ogonim's death and the end of the marriage to Adizua the cycle of rituals and conventions resumes with the marriage to Gilbert (Eneberi), and these are subsequently followed by the ceremonies in which Efuru is dedicated to Uhamiri and in which she formally separates from Gilbert by ritualistically disproving his capricious accusation of adultery.

This series of ceremonies is centered on that body-consciousness which is so pervasive in Nwapa's fiction. Her women are extremely conscious of their bodies in relation to their roles as wives and mothers. Accordingly, most of the prescribed rites in which Efuru participates are as physically oriented as they are morally justified. Clitoridectomy, for example, is both physically "useful" (allegedly, to facilitate child birth) and a morally sanctioned compliance with established religious and social custom. The total effect of this pervasive and intense body-consciousness among the women is to encourage the acceptance of their roles as inevitable and necessary. As Ossai assures her daughter-in-law Efuru, the excruciating pain of a clitoridectomy has to be accepted because the rite is every woman's lot (p. 12).

Even the ceremonial test of adultery charges which precipitate Efuru's separation from Gilbert is based on a certain preoccupation with the woman's body, for the test is designed to prove or disprove Efuru's declaration that no other man, apart from her husband, has seen her thighs (p. 280). Conversely, Efuru's ceremonial initiation and experiences as a worshipper of Uhamiri encourage a certain distance from those biological preoccupations which seem inherent in the perception of the woman as wife and mother. As a worshipper she is forbidden to sleep with her husband on Orie (the deity's holy day), and her physical separateness emphasizes the growing self-sufficiency that is symbolized by the Uhamiri figure. As she is freed from the biologically based conventions of marriage and motherhood, Efuru is progressively attracted towards a questioning, even subversive, rationalism. It is more than coincidental that it is on Orie night (when she is released from the physical responsibilities of marriage) that she is most aware of her own ideas. She believes she is becoming more logical in her reasoning, even though she thinks that it is unusual for women to be logical rather than intuitive (p. 208).

The series of ceremonies and conventions documents Efuru's growth into, and then away from, the traditional roles of wife and mother, and although her eventual independence is actually sanctioned by her community's traditions, her situation is not really paradoxical. The course of her development demonstrates how her society is able to accommodate personal needs and communal conventions whenever the necessity arises. This kind of accommodation or coexistence takes place within Efuru herself. In her personality, the earlier loyalty to the customary roles of wife and mother had existed side by side with a certain scepticism about the common assumption that established wisdom (regarding the *need* to choose motherhood) is inviolate, and that the woman must always heed that wisdom. In retrospect, her eventual decision to be a single, childless woman is really the logical outcome of a spirited individualism that has always been part of her temperament even when she was involved in marriage and motherhood and in the conventions, or ceremonies, which sustain those roles.

The first comment on her personality ("She was a remarkable woman") actually pinpoints her unusual self-assertiveness (p. 1). It is at her insistence that Adizua and herself live together without first observing the usual formalities of parental consent, bride price, circumcision (clitoridectomy), and so forth. Whenever it seems irrelevant to her needs and personal integrity she is frankly indifferent to that massive public opinion which represents the community in the dialogue structure of the novel:

"Did I hear that you have left your husband [Adizua]?"
"Yes, he has left me."
"Don't say that my daughter, don't say that. We say that a woman has left her husband, but never say that a husband has left his wife. Wives leave husbands not the other way around."
Efuru began to laugh. "It is the same thing to me" (p. 111).

Once again, this individualism actually coexists with Efuru's deep loyalty to those communal traditions which do not seem irrelevant or restrictive to her. In spite of that initial disregard for the formalities of betrothal and marriage, she does not really feel "married" to Adizua until those rites have been performed (p. 23).

The combination of conformity and rebelliousness in Efuru's personality is not only comparable with her society's accommodation of the conventional and the independent woman, it also corresponds with the diversity of her friendships. Her closest friend Ajanupu embodies that strength of will and that fiercely independent spirit into which Efuru herself is growing. Ajanupu's own unmatched skills as a mother (she is Efuru's chief counsellor in this regard) is combined with a strong individualism that brooks no affront from other women—or from men, as Gilbert discovers to his cost when she clubs him to the ground during a quarrel. On the other hand, Ajanupu's sister Ossai (Efuru's mother-in-law) who is also a close friend of Efuru, lacks that pugnacious spirit which characterizes Ajanupu. Ossai bears misfortunes (like her husband's neglect) meekly whereas Ajanupu is more strong-willed and less likely to surrender to adversity (p. 96).

Efuru's friendships reflect on her self-awareness as an individual. The sisters Ajanupu and Ossai represent the two distinct choices—independence or excessive submissiveness—which Efuru faces in her own life. At the same time her self-awareness, in relation to such choices, brings Efuru face to face with the fundamental implications of change in her private self as woman, in her community as a whole, and in the universal patterns of time itself. When she returns to her father's house from the broken marriage with Gilbert she observes that she has actually ended where she began—in her father's house (p. 280). However, she does not really end exactly where she began. Her father's death and her divorce have accentuated the external image of aloneness and independence, and her inner growth since she left her father's house to live with her first husband lends substance to that public image. Her experience has been both cyclical and progressive: there has been the cycle of rituals which formally prepared her for and initiated her into womanhood, and there have been the repetitive cycles of birth, life, and death which have made her aware of time itself as a process of constant change and growth; but as a direct result of these cycles, Efuru has grown, or progressed, from a dependence on the institutions represented by some of these cycles (especially marriage and motherhood) to a fully developed independence.

Here, too, Efuru's personality and experience are symptomatic of her own community as a whole. The novel's structure enforces a sense of continuing and multiple cycles in the communal experience. The rituals of betrothal, marriage, birth, and death are not only a form of individual education; they are also the community's collective and traditional response to the repetitive cycles of birth, growth, death, and burial which constitute time itself.

The body-consciousness which sustains the conventions of sexual roles is itself an expression of that communal response to time as life and death, change and growth; for the biological concerns of womanhood, the physical fragility of childhood and old age, and the phenomena of birth (Ogonim's) and death are all symptoms of time itself. Since experience is so closely related to the cycles of time, the actions of the individual and the rituals of the community are all consciously associated with specific cycles of time. Accordingly, some of the crucial events in Efuru's life are deliberately assigned to specific days. She elopes with Adizua on Nkwo day and makes plans for her circumcision on Nkwo day; or she makes peace with her father, after the elopement, on Eke day and subsequently gives thanks for Ogonim's birth on Eke day. Among the religious traditions, Orie day is sacred to Uhamiri. In general, the folk tale of Eke, Orie, Afo, and Nkwo (day names) reinforces the impression of time as a cyclical whole in Efuru's individual experience and in the communal experience at large.

That folk tale is one example of the oral modes Nwapa uses in order to convey the community's perception of time and experience in circular terms. The ubiquitous dialogue structure is another. The circumlocutory design of formal dialogues in the novel is not merely a rhetorical convention required by the community's norms of politeness. Neither is it simply a device for dramatic suspense and for instilling a sense of social or moral order. In addition to all of these, it also reflects the cyclical patterns which the community perceives in experience itself. The art of circumlocution (and it is nothing less than a highly developed art form among Nwapa's speakers) acquires an air of inevitability and repetitiveness from the speakers' skillfully polite repetition of familiar details. This is also true of the effects created by statement and refrain in the highly formal dialogues, on ceremonial occasions like the blessing of the infant Ogonim by the dibia. The cyclical effect of repetitiveness corresponds with those cycles of experience dominating the beliefs and oral discourse of the community:

"I have never caused any one to die."
"Ise."
"I have never prepared poison to kill anybody."

"That's how it happened," Adizua and Efuru said.

"I inherited all my medicines from my father, who inherited them from his father."

"Ise," they nodded.

"Our family is upright, and fear God. So God see to it that our enemies are crushed."

"Ise."

"Let Ogonim live long."

"Ise."

"Let Efuru have one baby, one baby until the house is full."

"Ise." (pp. 36-37).

As in Efuru's case, the community's perception of time as a cycle exists side by side with community's experience of time and change as historical progression. The cyclical image of birth-life-death is apparent in events like the dibia's prophecy of more children for Efuru, his own death shortly afterwards, Ogonim's death and Efuru's subsequent childlessness. Simultaneously, a non-cyclical, progressive change is signified, in Efuru's life, by her withdrawal from the motherhood role. Her father's death is both intrinsic to the eternal life-death cycle and symbolic of noncyclical historical changes in his society, for his death marks the passing of a generation that played a crucial role in past events (slavery and colonialism) which profoundly and permanently changed the course of African history (p. 258). The universal and eternal cycles of life and death coexist with specific and temporal changes within the community. If society can experience these specific historical changes while observing those lasting cylces of life and death, so can an individual member of the society, such as Efuru, grow into a special kind of aloneness and independence without necessarily destroying the cyclical wholeness of the communal traditions and structures.

Efuru's final choice does not actually deny the validity of communal tradition as such, but it does demonstrate (1) the need of a certain kind of woman to establish her independence within the community, and (2) the capacity of the community to accommodate that need. The crucial issue in Efuru's development is the matter of choice. Musing on her alter ego, the Woman of the Lake, Efuru notes that the deity is wealthy, beautiful, and happy, that she bestows these gifts on women, and yet she was childless. Why, Efuru asks, do women worship a deity who had never experienced the "joys" of motherhood? (p. 281). This question, the concluding statement of the novel, is really rhetorical: women like Efuru who tend to be self-sufficient worship the Woman of the Lake because she represents what they have chosen to be. Faced with two choices —marriage and motherhood on the one hand, and independence on the other hand—Efuru elects a course that is suitable to her needs without breaking her relationship with the community as a whole. The emphasis is not on specific roles, but on the woman's need for a free choice of roles.

This question of choice is also the underlying theme of *Idu*. In Idu's community the familiar ideal of motherhood is an insistent and recurrent refrain in the lives of women who publicly define their very existence exclusively in terms of childbearing: "What we are all praying for is children. What else do we want if we have children?" (p. 150). Idu's story is really a reply to that question. She does have a child, but when her husband Adiewere dies she wills herself to die. In so doing she elects to continue the happy and fulfilling marriage after death rather than to live on as a mother. Idu does not assume that a husband is indispensable for a woman's self-respect, any more than she accepts the consensus that motherhood is the only significant justification for a woman's existence. Her final choice emphasizes that it is the matter of choice itself that is most important in the woman's identity. Nwapa's protagonist arrives at her crucial decisions as individual in a social context that is heavily influenced by that sense of order which flows from strong social institutions and established moral norms—especially the conventions governing the woman's role as part of the family unit.

Indeed the family is not simply a social institution, but a moral force by which individuals may be judged. Adiewere supports his shiftless brother Ishiodu largely in response to the moral obligations of family ties. Conversely, when Idu's younger sister Anamadi remains indifferent to family responsibilities she threatens the order of the unit, just as her frequent quarrels outside the home threaten both the social order as a whole and the family's relationship with the society. Idu and Adiewere are dissociated from the self-seeking individualism of Ishiodu and Anamadi while pursuing a measure of personal fulfillment that departs to a degree from the community's most cherished ideals of marriage and parenthood. As in the case of Efuru, their individual choices as man and woman are developed within, rather than at the expense of, the communal order. Their insistence on private needs and preferences goes hand in hand with a deep respect for the communal ideal. Idu is comparable with Efuru who flouts the conventions of betrothal and bride price but does not feel truly married until she has finally observed them. In Idu's case, notwithstanding her eventual choice of death over motherhood, she never felt adequate as a woman until she had given birth to a child (p. 47).

Although the moral significance of social conventions is about equal in the two novels, one senses in *Idu* that there are greater emotional pressures on the individual to conform with the community's ideals of sexual roles and parenthood. The pressure is both external and internal, accentuated on the outside by the pervasive role of dialogues as the vehicle of communal viewpoints, and emphasized from within by an urgently personal awareness (especially in Idu's case) of choices between life and death. The communal viewpoint seems to be more insistent and audible than in *Efuru*, not simply because the narrative structure relies more heavily on the dialogue form, but because in this work Nwapa organizes most of the dialogues around a small group of speakers rather than distributing them among several groups. Nwasobi and her friend Uzoechi share the main burden of this communal commentary, with one or the other occasionally giving way to a central character like Idu. The total effect of this technique is to endow the community's viewpoint with a personal presence that is derived from the familiarity, and frequent appearance, of the same commentators. When an unpleasant member of the community like Oyenmuru offers a comment, her judgement derives a certain force from what we already know of her character. Her remarks about the isolation and bereavement that follow death are the more authoritative because Oyenmuru's unpleasant personality has resulted in her being the most isolated person in her village.

Altogether Nwasobi and Uzoechi, and their occasional substitutes, serve as a chorus, in the manner of the drama. This choral structure imparts to the communal viewpoint a weighty authority which contributes to the formidable communal pressures upon the individual. The authority of the chorus is linked not only with its roots in the community, but with its repeated emphasis on the decisive role of fate or destiny in the experience of community and individual alike. It is Nwasobi, for example, who reminds Idu about the universal inevitability of death (p. 125). The role of the chorus in emphasizing universal destiny (death, for example) is paralleled by its function in defining social "fate" or roles (such as motherhood). This parallel is highly appropriate in the novel since the question of social roles (especially sexual roles) poses universal, life-or-death choices for individuals like Idu and others in her society. Consequently, when Idu's friend Ojiugo finds that her husband is sterile she has no qualms about deserting him for a man who can guarantee her the cherished role of mother. Appropriately, it is the chorus of Nwasobi and Uzoechi that announces this communally oriented choice. The suspenseful structure and repetitive patterns of their dialogue heighten the sense of inevitability and strengthen the impression of an authoritative order which has made Ojiugo's decision both natural and predictable:

"Come, come, do you know? Do you know that Ojiugo has left her husband?" Nwasobi asked her friend Uzoechi.
"Who said so? It is a lie. It cannot happen. Ojiugo can't have left her husband."
"I am telling you it is true. Haven't you heard? She has left Amarajeme."
"You don't know what you are saying. Don't repeat it, or else the gods will hear. Left him for whom? . . . Who has she gone to now? Did Amarajeme ill-treat her?" asked Uzoechi.
"He did not. It is foolishness, that's all."
"Who has she gone to, that's what I am asking," Uzoechi insisted.
"To Obukodi. . . . "
"I don't know what Ojiugo wants in Obukodi's house. What does she want? Is it because she has no child by Amarajeme?" asked Uzoechi.
"Of course, what else?" asked Nwasobi (pp. 104-105).

Amarajeme chooses death by hanging when it is no longer possible to doubt his inability to be a father, but there is very little similarity between Amarajeme's suicide and Idu's subsequent act of willing herself to die. He chooses death, not because he regrets the loss of a beloved wife, but because her desertion and her pregnancy by another man bring into the open the fact that he is sterile. In choosing death, he accepts the community's overriding concern with motherhood and fatherhood. On the other hand, Idu is already a mother when she dies, and her death signifies her rejection of the community's consensus that motherhood is the only justification for a woman's life. Unlike most women who, according to Nwasobi and Uzoechi, pray for children, Idu prays for life, as she remarks to Amarajeme on one occasion (p. 206). Idu's choice of life, of a qualitatively satisfying life, springs in part from an awareness of the essential fragility of life itself. Her passionate commitment to the quality of her life with Adiewere renders death itself relatively insignificant: it merely represents the transformation of the context within which their love will continue. Once Adiewere crosses the stream to the land of the dead, it only remains for her to follow him so that they can continue the relationship (p. 210). This is the basis on which she declines to enter upon formal mourning for Adiewere, detaching herself in the process from another set of orally defined conventions in her community. She turns her back on a custom that is rooted in established, socially sanctioned roles (wife and bereaved widow), emphasizing instead those personal feelings which go beyond social conventions, and beyond easy distinctions between life and death.

The triumphant effect of Idu's choice and her minimizing of death is particularly strong because the themes and tone of the novel have been so dominated up to that point by the presence of death. When the opening dialogue of the narrative announces that Adiewere is ill, it introduces a note of foreboding that hangs over the story to the end. There are insistent reminders of the role of death in the very continuity of life itself, especially when Adiewere's sister-in-law Ogbenyanu almost dies of a miscarriage (pp. 17-18), a friend suddenly dies of rabies (pp. 57-59), Amarajeme hangs himself (p. 143), and the eclipse of the sun offers a terrifying symbol of the life-death cycle itself, with light (life) giving way to darkness (death) which, just as inevitably, gives way to life again (p. 84). The symbolism of that eclipse touches Idu in a very personal way: she gives birth to a child (after the "death" of years of childlessness) during the sun's temporary "death," thereby enforcing the theme of death and life as coexistent realities. The life-death-life sequence which the eclipse symbolically outlines, anticipates the sequence of Idu's happy life with her husband, the temporary, eclipsing effects of his death, and finally her triumphant affirmation, by her own death, of the vital and fulfilling nature of that life.

In developing the "fate" of motherhood or childlessness, life or death, the themes and choral structure of the novel unfold on the basis of statement and response (or rebuttal). The dialogue-as-chorus introduces the theme of motherhood as the prerequisite of womanhood, and this thematic statement is rebutted by Idu's final choice. Similarly, ubiquitous emphases on death as final arbiter are countered by Idu's redefinition of death as a transforming alternative rather than decisive ending. This narrative pattern of statement-and-response corresponds with that most elemental of oral techniques in the folk tale—the kind of statement and response which the children in Idu's village employ for their stories and play songs during the harvest festival:

> Small bird, small bird
> *Turunziza nziza.*
> What are you doing in you nest?
> *Turunziza nziza.*
> I am preparing some sticks (p. 154).

The song proceeds to discover the ultimate motive, the small bird builds a house with sticks in order to lay eggs and to be "like others" in having children. The circular structure of statement and response reflects the cycle of birth-life-death upon which the play song itself is based: the experience of creation and life, family and birth links all levels of creation. The desire to be like others, the desire to be mothers, links the bird, the girls singing the song, and the community whose harvest festival celebrates life and creation on yet another level.

The circular pattern, and the cyclical themes, which are inherent in the statement-and-response of the folk tale or play song are also characteristic of the dialogue form in this novel. As in *Efuru*, the circular pattern of the dialogue is the major vehicle for describing the cyclical experience of birth, life, and death—especially as it affects the woman and her sense of choice. Even more insistently than in *Efuru*, the dialogue form in *Idu* invites comparison between its own structure (the circularity of statement, response and repetition) and theme. The opening dialogue between Nwasobi and Uzoechi is therefore the finest example of its kind in the work, because its basic narrative function (introducing the main characters, themes, and the speakers themselves) depends on the same circular, or circumlocutory, structure which also emphasizes the life-death cycle. That cycle is implied by their account of Adiewere's illness, Idu's childlessness, the couple's remarkably happy life together, and the community's prayers for Idu's pregnancy (pp. 1-3).

The speakers' fear of death and their emphasis on the couple's happy life amount to more than factual observations for the sake of introducing certain narrative details. They initiate a series of comments (which become increasingly ominous) on the interdependence and shared vitality of Idu and her husband. They point the dialogue itself in the direction of the narrative as a whole—towards Adiewere's death and Idu's subsequent choice. The dialogue reflects the cyclical structure of the novel as a whole—moving from polite everyday formalities (enquires about each other's health, for example), to a preoccupation with the cycle of life and death and those activities and institutions which are linked to the cycle (marriage, parenthood, birth, more marriages, and so forth). The dialogue anticipates the inexorable sequence of events that lead to Idu's choice in the face of social conventions and death.

This kind of anticipation is the more convincing because the act of foreshadowing the future in the present is itself intrinsic to the cyclical structure of time and experience. At this juncture, the integration of dialogue structure, narrative design, and theme is complete—and this kind of integration is a prime example of Nwapa's sure handling of oral modes within the design of her novel. This is generally true of both novels, but there is a discernible difference in *Idu*. The tone of this later novel is more somber. The cycles of life and death, and the communal presence which dominates the dialogue structure all seem to be more pressing and insistent. As a result there is a correspondingly greater sense of freedom in the startling nature of Idu's final choice.

The tight sense of organization and structure which serves Nwapa so well in her fiction, including the short stories, seems particularly striking and effective in *Idu* because it enforces our sense of a tightly knit, even suffocating, communality in Idu's world. There is no real rejection of that communal value system in the work as a whole, and this novel is as much a celebration of the system's dignity and strengths as is *Efuru*. However, the barely disguised tensions between an admirable, supportive community and an individuality that seeks some independence, some breathing room, are more pronounced in the second novel. There is a fundamental dilemma here, one that has been clear since *Efuru*. How does one achieve that kind of independence while supporting and functioning within such a closely knit communal system? This dilemma is not really resolved in either novel. In *Efuru*, Nwapa goes around it by allowing Efuru an alternative which, while unusual when compared with the lives of most women, is still sanctioned by the community's religious and social traditions. In *Idu*, the dilemma is not solved, but met more squarely—and with rather more thought-provoking implications. Idu's choice of death can be seen positively, as an affirmation of love and a commitment to her husband that transcends death itself. On a more negative, rather covert level, it is clear that the choice also amounts to an escape—from the insistent voice of the community (which would have had her remarry and have children in this case), and from the potential or actual restrictiveness that this voice implies for her own sense of individuality.

Without rejecting the communal system, Idu manages to circumvent it in a way that satisfies her pesonal needs rather than the community's overriding criteria (marriage and motherhood). The community's value system remains intact—at least, they are not overtly challenged, and in the process Idu is able to have her own way. What we have is a balancing act by Nwapa. The communal system continues, but individuals like Idu are being allowed more room than even Efuru to exercise their own eccentric sense of need or choice—as long as that eccentricity does not outrage or disrupt the communal order. On balance, *Idu* falls somewhere between the frank espousal of the communal tradition in Sutherland's drama and the Western-oriented sense of individualism in the novels of South Africa's Bessie Head.

7   Bessie Head

Like many other black South African writers, Bessie Head lives in exile from South Africa. Her chosen place of exile is neighboring Botswana, where she has lived since 1964, "as a stateless person," in her words, who is required to register with the local police.[1] Her three novels are set in Botswana, and her themes reflect the exile's prevailing sense of homelessness.[2] But in its most profound sense, Head's fiction draws significantly upon the experience of being a nonwhite in South Africa, for the denial of civil rights to the South African nonwhite encourages Head's sense of homelessness in much the same way that the system of apartheid fragments the individual's sense of personal integrity. Physical exile and the permanent status as a refugee in Botswana are not distinguished, in Head's fiction, from the stateless condition which South Africa represents for nonwhites living in that country. Indeed, Head's personal background confirms this symbolism. She was born in an asylum for the insane to a white woman who had been placed in the institution for having dared to become pregnant by Bessie's black father, and her enforced condition as orphan is an intrinsic part of a continuing experience which has denied her a national identity in southern Africa, especially in Botswana and South Africa.

Head's racial experience as a South African "colored" (to borrow the quaint South African designation for racially mixed persons) has encouraged a profound alienation from prevailing ethical traditions and from many existing social institutions. This rebelliousness goes hand in hand with a certain scepticism about what she sees as the special disadvantages of women. This scepticism inspires a search, in her novels, for humane sexual roles and political values within a harmonious social order. In her fiction, the limitations of the woman's role and self-image, and the historical dispossession of the nonwhite are the very essence of a pervasive social malaise. In Head's view, that malaise assumes the proportions of a far-ranging moral crisis: racism, sexism, poverty, and entrenched social inequities are both the special ills of her world in southern Africa and the symptoms of a universal moral disorder. This revulsion at the moral wasteland of her world has also inspired an intensely moral idealism, one that assumes the force of a crusade in her fiction, sparking the quest for a more creative and less power-hungry sense of self. Head's work as a writer is closely integrated with her personal life in Botswana, for she has chosen to live in a rural village, working in a farming cooperative in which political refugees of all kinds and colors attempt to develop a thriving community out of Botswana's unpromising terrain—creating, in Head's words, "new worlds out of nothing."[3]

All of this has combined to make Head a rather unique figure in the literature of southern Africa and in black African literature as a whole. She is the only nonwhite South African woman writing in English to deal at length and in any significant terms with sexual roles and racial identity as they are related to each other, and as they represent the author's view of the world at large. There is a special bleakness in Head's moral vision and world view, one that seems to have been stimulated by an intense sense of isolation that is not found in the other writers discussed. West African writers like Sutherland, Aidoo, and Nwapa communicate a fairly comfortable sense of belonging, even when they raise questions about shortcomings or conflicts in their respective societies. They enjoy fairly close ties with tribal institutions and indigenuous customs, even when they are critical of aspects of those institutions and customs and even when they fear that they are disappearing under the impact of Western culture (Buchi Emecheta is alienated from her Ibo-Nigerian culture, but she conveys the impression of a relatively close identification with the West). As a South African "colored," Head is the perennial and archetypal outsider. The circumstances of her birth and upbringing cut her off from contact with her black African sources, but having inherited the civilization of the Christian West she has had to remain the West's historically unwanted offspring. Consequently, although she clearly recognizes the history of racial dispossession which she has shared with all blacks, this total alienation leaves her without strong ethnic loyalties, without the West African writer's complex grasp of the strengths and weaknesses of traditional African cultures.

This complete statelessness, or uprootedness, has tended to make Head the supremely alienated individual. She is deeply suspicious of all prevailing traditions and institutions, since she associates them with the widespread disorder she encounters in her world. Untempered by loyalty to ethnic group or region, this suspicion has no room for that recognition of saving graces which the reader will encounter in the social themes of the West African writers. There is, consequently, a greater urgency in Head's fiction to create "new worlds" of new men and women out of the nothing of the status quo. Predictably, this kind of moral intensity leads to some unevenness in Head's work. Her single most consistent weakness is a tendency to oversimplify complex social and ethnic experiences by way of a straightforward, singleminded didacticism that makes no distinction between racial consciousness as destructive racism and racial consciousness as a creative, even integrative, awareness of one's self and group and of another's ethnic identity. In attacking the power-centered brutishness which often characterizes most male-female relationships, her moral sensors often seem to confuse sexual passion per se with the manipulative violence that often substitutes for sexual love.

In spite of these shortcomings, her moral idealism remains the most powerfully effective and most distinguishing feature of her three novels—*When Rain Clouds Gather* (1968), *Maru* (1971) and *A Question of Power* (1974). Her idealism nurtures her strengths as a realistic novelist, enabling her to turn uprootedness into a vantage point from which she scrutinizes social institutions as they usually are—as they distort individual personality through power-oriented definitions of race, sex, religion, and individualism. Whenever she is not being merely didactic, this moral intensity makes for a vigorous directness in her description of social systems as they exist in her society. An even more impressive strength consists of her ability to create or suggest possibilities for new worlds in her fictive milieu, while at the same time insisting on the persistence of destructive traditions of power both in that milieu and in the world that it imitates. Throughout her fiction she maintains the kind of narrative irony that results from the continuous tension between a fervent idealism and a frank, sometimes brutal, realism. This blend of the ideal and the actual, especially with regards to the issues of power and identity, has had the effect of making her novels the most ambitious by an African woman, especially with regard to novels that deal with the condition of women against the turbulent background of contemporary Africa.

There are clear signs of this ambition in the first novel, *When Rain Clouds Gather*. It describes the usual experiences of exile, the refugee in this case being Makhaya, a young Zulu who has fled into Botswana in order to escape prosecution for anti-apartheid activities in South Africa. He settles in the small village of Golema Mmidi where he becomes an important member of an agricultural cooperative operated by the local people and a number of other refugees. His closest friends in the cooperative are Paulina Sebeso, whom he eventually marries, Gilbert Balfour, a British agronomist who heads the cooperative, and Gilbert's wife Maria, the daughter of a local elder. The plot, like those of the two subsequent novels, is quite loose and is centered on the various stages of the cooperative's development. That development proceeds against a number of obstacles—the ingrained conservatism of the local people and their suspicion of new techniques; a reactionary chief who is jealous of the cooperative's encroachment on his traditional privileges; a severe drought which decimates the local cattle population; and the insecurities within, or barriers between, the members of the cooperative.

The plot clearly recalls Head's personal experiences as a new refugee in Botswana. The cooperative represents the creation of a new world, or the possibilities of creating a new world, from the nothingness of Botswana's harsh landscape and from the destructiveness of the refugees' past. Makhaya's success in the cooperative heralds a new purposiveness in the community, an outlook that replaces the disillusionment and self-destructive hatred with which he first enters Golema Mmidi. His eventual union with Paulina (herself a refugee from a disastrous marriage in northern Botswana) symbolizes the kind of harmony in which sexual equality is intrinsic to individual growth and socio-economic achievement.

Unfortunately, the moral idealism which shapes this vision of new worlds and renewed human beings is also the source of weaknesses that also appear in later works. The novelist's didacticism sometimes strains her credibility. When that rambunctious reactionary, Chief Matenge, is struck down by high blood pressure, after unsuccessfully trying to destroy the cooperative, the moral apparatus of punishment and reward is too obvious and contrived. When that same apparatus turns up at the end to dispose of the chief by way of an unlikely suicide, it weakens the effectiveness of the novel's conclusion. The moral condemnation of divisive customs and repressive institutions is consistent for the most part, and generally persuasive, but sometimes it is developed simplistically. When this happens it raises questions about Head's historical sense and about the depth of her social perspectives. Tribal traditions, for example, are always seen in wholly negative terms—as narrow conservatism and stultifying oppressiveness, as a system based only on the manipulation of "meek sheep" by illiterate rulers (p. 43).

In a similar vein, the rise of nationalism and positive racial self-awareness in black Africa is simply equated with South African apartheid or with the tribal feudalism of Chief Matenge. The one-dimensional images of ethnic awareness (mere racism), tribal traditions (parochial backwardness), and cultural nationalism (a Pan-African counterpart to apartheid) compromise her moral judgements. These judgements depend too heavily on an obviously limited perspective that defines institutions and traditions solely on the basis on which they have historically been corrupted. In Head's fiction one does not often find the kind of complex political awareness that marks someone like Ghana's Sutherland. Instead, we are left with an odd contradiction. The novelist seems unable to envision cultural or ethnic awareness per se as part of an ideally harmonious world, but at the same time she insists that individualism as such need not be mere selfishness, as it often is, but can be fundamental to the kind of moral growth that facilitates sexual and social harmony. Oddly enough, this ability to see individualism both as traditional evil and as potential good has no counterpart in her handling of ethnic or national consciousness.

Finally, the limitations of the novelist's moral judgements some-time coincide with the thinness and disturbing conventionality of ethical terms. The use of "black" as a maledictive term (the "black" rage of Paulina's sexual jealousy, for example) is not only trite. It is an example of traditional (Western) symbolism, one that is par-ticularly incongruous in a work that repeatedly attacks the racial and political manipulation of language—the white man's reference to blacks as "kaffirs," "boys," and "dogs," for example.

This kind of conventionality tends to stand out in *Rain Clouds* precisely because the work demonstrates an imaginative power and an original grasp of style which lend compelling force to Head's moral vision. The description of the drought-stricken lands from which the cooperative must wrest some life is Head at her best:

> It was just as though everything was about to die. The small brown birds had deserted the bush, and the bush itself no longer supplied the coverage and protection for the secret activities of the scarlet and golden birds. Here and there, faint patches of green clung to the topmost branches of tall thorn trees, but not a green thing survived near the sun-baked earth. The sky had lost that dense blue of the winter days and spread itself out into a whitish film. . . . In this desolation the vultures reigned supreme.
>   . . . . Now, the vultures, full and gorged, adorned the bare trees, and beneath their resting places lay the white, picked bones of the dead cattle (pp. 166, 168).

The arresting images of death and decay have assumed cosmic proportions—the drought represents a widespread moral malaise—and they blend easily with the harsh moral landscape of the novel as a whole. It is a landscape that is marked by division and by the fragmenting abuse of power. The barbed wire fence through which Makhaya crosses into Botswana is a graphic symbol of racial separation and international distrust. The disease and poverty which kill Paulina's ten year-old son during the drought symbolize a poverty of spirit in a society in which suspicion and powerful privilege (in the person of corrupt rulers) sometimes thwart social harmony and stunt an individual sense of personal integrity. In general, the thematic development of the novel is based on the movement of the novelist's viewpoint, from a painfully realistic image of the social landscape as it is, to the vision of an ideal world based on individual growth and social harmony. On this basis, the cooperative is clearly the symbolic ideal that acts as counterweight to the implications of the vulture-infested landscape. It represents a healing moral growth, reflecting not only the creative purposeful-ness of individual members but also an unusual degree of harmony between the races and the sexes.

The cooperative's promise of social harmony is strengthened by the racial cooperation that is involved in the venture. Gilbert, the trained agronomist, represents the best of scientific rationalism in the white West, the kind of rationalism that is aimed at improve-ment, rather than brutalization, of human beings, and in the co-operative this rationalism merges with the African emphasis on people. The result is an impression of wholeness that is further strengthened by the cosmic implications of the cooperative's literal investment in the soil, in the land itself. Wresting food and abun-dance from a grudging environment is an act of creation in a uni-versal sense, one that is profoundly spiritual as well as physical. Even the doggedly pragmatic Gilbert recognizes that agriculture and the idea of a Deity are intrinsically intertwined, each being symptoms of a universal creative power (p. 184). For its members, the cooperative is also a "strange gathering of wills" (p. 192), a creative union that is powerful enough to achieve the material goals of harvest from an arid land, and spiritually decisive enough to drive a corrupt chief into despair and suicide. By virtue of its creative function and harmonizing energies the cooperative resembles the godhead itself, encompassing the small birds of the bush, the dusty footpaths of the village and the "expressions of thin old men in tattered coats" (p. 195).

Makhaya's own experience corresponds with the symbolism of the cooperative and his personality is presented as one that grows into a creative and harmonizing kind of force. His flight from South Africa and quest for a new home in Botswana endows the novel as a whole with a narrative sense of movement which, in turn, heightens our awareness of *progressive* changes in his charac-ter. In Makhaya's personal odyssey, the idea of change is trans-formed from mere escape into dynamic growth. He begins as an extremely alienated person with a single-minded determination to be free of South Africa and to be uninvolved with all human beings thereafter. His participation in the cooperative leads to a compassionate concern on his part for others—for the future of Botswana, Africa, and the rest of humanity. His "inner life," to borrow Head's favorite phrase, begins to respond to the harmony of the cooperative after years of hatred and internal conflict, and this kind of response centers on his growing sexual involvement with Paulina. His earlier contempt for his Zulu name and its meaning (one who stays home) is modified when his sense of complete uprootedness, or statelessness, is replaced by a commitment to Paulina and to the community they are building.

Makhaya has no illusions about the fragile nature of the utopia that is being created at Golema Mmidi. The political and emotional upheavals of his own past have made him very aware that Golema Mmidi is the startling exception rather than the rule in his world, that it is really a refuge of sorts from the prevailing realities of the urban world. Makhaya has grown into a dual perception of his world, one which combines an idealistic perception of positive possibilities like Golema Mmidi, with a realistic awareness of much of the world as it actually is. His character reflects the highly effective tension, in Head's narrative viewpoint, between the visionary and the sceptic.

This kind of tension is most pronounced in Head's handling of those sexual themes which dominate the motif of growth in the novel. At their traditional worst, sexual relationships in the novel reflect established attitudes and institutions that have warped the individuality of both men and women. On the other hand, there is a movement (especially in the relationships between Makhaya and Paulina, Maria and Gilbert) towards sexual experience based on mutual respect and shared equality. In these sexual relationships, Head develops highly personal examples of that love and generosity which mark the regeneration of Golema Mmidi as a whole. At the same time, even these fulfilling and humane relationships are touched by the persistent influence of limiting ideas about sexuality and social roles. In the final analysis, the new women and men of Golema Mmidi are as ambiguous as the utopian world that they seem to be creating. The woman's identity is fundamental to all of this. It reflects the roles of established conventions in this part of southern Africa, roles which Head scornfully dismisses as "old tribal selves, docile and inferior'' (p. 69) and which are deprived, in modern Africa, even of the old protective customs that once existed for women (p. 123). On the other hand, the new possibilities, represented by Golema Mmidi, also imply new choices and expanded roles for women as equal partners in the new community.

In this connection, Paulina Seboso is one of those strong person-alities, in both sexes, who play a decisive role in the development of the cooperative, and she is crucial in ensuring the full participation of women in the new order of things. This pioneering energy is complemented by the fact that as a refugee she shares with other newcomers the image of rebelliousness against the status quo, and since she has left an unsuccessful marriage behind in nothern Bots-wana, her rebellion has specific sexual implications that touch upon her identity as a woman. As a leader against subordinating con-ventions she quickly encourages the women of Golema Mmidi to participate in the cooperative as full equals. She is also a uniquely ''new'' woman in the overall context of Head's narrative: her leadership qualities and the adventuresomeness which accompanies them distinguish her from other women, and her general assertive-ness discomfits what the narrator ridicules as ''effeminate shadows of men who really feared women'' (p. 95).

On balance, Paulina is not new in a complete sense. Her person-ality still bears the marks of the old conventions of female sub-ordination. Thus, from time to time, even her vigorous independence gives way to submissiveness in the company of strong male per-sonalities like Makhaya, and despite her prominence in the fight against rigidly defined roles, the old habits are still strong enough for her to be disturbed when Makhaya elects to do the ''woman's work'' of making a fire (p. 144). Her personality is very similar to Maria's, in that the latter combines a traditionally soft ''feminine'' demeanor with a ruthless commonsense that is impatient of restric-tive role-definitions. In effect, both women embody the ambiguities of the state of becoming: the influence of conventional roles persists side by side with a questioning, assertive sense of self and equality.

Their male counterparts represent similar ambiguities. Maria's split consciousness as a woman is matched by Gilbert's male duality. On one hand, he scorns the anemic feudal structures of class and sex in his native England, but on the other, in those moments in which Maria displays her spirited common sense, he automatically reverts to the standard notions of masculine prerogative. This kind of ambiguity is even more pronounced in the proportionately more rebellious Makhaya. His rebellion against social systems is intensified in a very personal way by his sexual preferences. He loathes the customary ideal of female submissiveness, partly because this kind of subordination conforms with those general patterns of inequality and repressiveness which he deplores in society as a whole, and partly because his own sexual and intellectual needs cannot be satisfied by the limited individualism which he encounters in conventionally subordinated women. In this regard he is clearly the embodiment of the (novelist's) feminist ideal of manhood. His ideas of maleness and femaleness are based on criteria of equality and interdependence rather than on conventional sanctions of masculine power and privilege, and his revolt against those conventional sanctions is integral to a broader rebellion against established patterns of domination and manipulation.

His eventual union with Paulina symbolically integrates the sexual revolt with the political rebellion. Her impatience with an insecure, overly aggressive masculinity is matched by his contempt for weak, conniving women. Their sexual union therefore not only celebrates the individual maturity into which they are both growing, it also represents the kind of broader social harmony that their relationship promises for the future society. That promise is not entirely fulfilled. Like Paulina, Makhaya is still loyal to aspects of the old value system, even at intense moments of rebellion. Notwithstanding his passionate commitment to sexual equality, his masculine ego is traditional enough for him to be relieved by the discovery that he is a foot taller than the formidable Paulina (p. 113). In moments of crisis (such as the death of Paulina's son) he is quite capable of compelling her to accept his help by lapsing into the man's traditional language and gestures, of protective, and dominating, leadership. He has arrived in her life, he advises her, to assume her burdens and responsibilities (p. 170).

It is typical of Makhaya's honesty, especially to himself, that he frankly acknowledges his paradoxical role. He is the domineering male enforcer of female equality. That frankness encourages the reader to see the apparent contradiction, not as mere hypocrisy, but as the ambiguities that are intrinsic to a period of transition and incomplete growth. There are also significant implications, for Head's own moral idealism, about male leadership in the cooperative (all the women are equal partners but it is directed by Makhaya and Gilbert), and in the process of changing old sexual roles. The idealist's vision of a new world of sexual equality is tempered by a wryly realistic insistence on the fact that old values can persist into the new world while it is being created.

The novel insists on the very real limitations which strongly entrenched habits impose upon attempts at change. Moreover the creation of new institutions or social values depends on personal growth, on that maturity of the inner self which is a prerequisite for any general rebirth in society at large. Visions of new social systems and ethical values are easy enough, but in Head's fiction these visions are counterbalanced by a level-headed and sometimes deliberately discouraging emphasis on the conflicts within the individual's inner self. Implicit in all of this is Head's awareness of the tendency among idealistic reformers to launch crusades for public changes while ignoring the highly private and inner rehabilitation upon which collective reform depends. The successful creation of a "new world" at Golema Mmidi, and in the human condition at large, therefore depends on the ability of individuals like Makhaya and Paulina to experience completely the kind of rigorous self-exploration and self-rehabilitation that is centered on the private or inner self. As the ultimate source of new social possibilities, this interior vision or self-knowledge becomes a crucial force in Head's fiction. It is a power that is at once destructively conventional and creatively rebellious, and, in this respect, it explains the ambiguity and sense of incompleteness that surround even growing personalities like Makhaya and Paulina.

This inner power fascinates Head on another basis. It is intensely individual and private, but at the same time it is the absolute prerequisite, in its humane form, for the achievment of public harmony based on social justice. In this regard the individual's own self-knowledge is analogous to the artistic imagination itself—highly idiosyncratic in form and expression, but symbolic of and commited to the artist's community. Like the individual need to envision a sense of wholeness and creativity in the very midst of chaos and fragmentation, art reflects a capacity to visualize life even in the midst of death and to visualize harmony in the experience of conflict. This aspect of the artistic imagination is not simply analogous to the moral creativity of the individual's inner self, it is actually one manifestation of its power. Paulina's son carves breathtakingly beautiful works of art even as he dies of tuberculosis in a drought-striken wasteland, and conversely that very wasteland is the symbolic setting in which Paulina and Makhaya discover the development of that inner strength which is to be the basis of their sexual relationship.

Head does not allow her reader the dubious luxury of celebrating art and inner self as unfailing and supreme powers in the creation of some new order. The pervasive deathliness of the Botswana wasteland and the death of the child-artist enforce a sense of fragility and limitations. The artist's morally ideal and socially harmonious vision is counterbalanced by the harsh realities of the artist's environment. Like the individual's dream of sexual equality and socioeconomic utopias, the artistic imagination is important not because it can guarantee the realization of what it envisions, but because the very capacity for ideal visions is the symptom of a creative power or moral energy that already exists within the individual's inner self. Without offering easy promises about the imminent passing of the wasteland, the artist's reminder of the power of the inner self constitutes a splendid defiance of the wasteland.

This undercurrent of realism in her handling of the artistic imagination and social reform also explains why Head insists on the isolation and uniqueness of Golema Mmidi. The events there represent a highly unusual attempt to reject established norms of sex, race, and politics in their entirety, and this very uniqueness or isolation sharply qualifies the applicability of Golema Mmidi— even as a half developed and tentative utopia—to the world at large. This qualification is a telling comment on the world outside Golema Mmidi. Clearly, the realism which tempers her moral idealism also lends a special pointedness to Head's satiric view of the world. The shortcomings of society and individuals are accentuated by the very idealism that they inspire in an onlooker like Head, but the promise of new growth is limited by the persistence of the moral drought. All good things and people are called rain, Paulina reminds Makhaya during the hot dry weather. We see rain clouds gather, she adds, even when the sky is actually cloudless (pp. 176-77). In other words, moral idealism is actually an imaginative response to the harsh realities of the world as it is. The gathering of the rain clouds—the promise of good things and people—is therefore not a guaranteed reality. It is a symptom of that moral and imaginative power which demonstrates the strength of the inner self.

The person and imagination of the artist occupy a more central position in Head's second novel. In *Maru* the main protagonist, Margaret Cadmore, is an artist, and we view most of the narrative events through her eyes. She is a member of the despised Masarwa tribe of Botswana, and she has been named after the British missionary who adopted her. The use of Margaret as a major narrative medium endows *Maru* with a degree of subjective unity, and in this respect the novel represents a significant shift from the multiple viewpoints (Makhaya, Paulina and others) of *Rain Clouds*. This shift corresponds with Head's increasing concentration on the inner awareness of the individual woman and artist. *Maru* reflects Head's greater involvement in questions about the nature of art and the significance of power (social and psychological), not only on their own terms but also with respect to the woman's experience.

These questions are inherent in Margaret's situation as a school teacher in the village of Dilepe where she faces the usual tribal prejudices against Masarwas. She is befriended by Maru and Moleka, both members of the ruling elite, and by Maru's sister Dikeledi. These three are depicted as progressives: their friendship with Margaret is a personal extension of their fight against social prejudices and political privileges in their community. The relationship is complicated by a double love triangle: both Moleka and Maru are in love with Margaret, and at the same time both Margaret and Dikeledi love Moleka who has a reputation as an insensitive and sexually exploitive young man. Relying on his power and prestige as chieftain, Maru encourages Moleka to seduce and then marry Dikeledi, and with his rival out of the way proceeds to elope with the disappointed Margaret, taking the latter on the proverbial rebound. The prevailing love themes of the novel do pose a technical problem for Head because of the awkwardness with which she usually handles personal intimacies of this kind. The imaginative power with which she can describe hatred, death, and poverty (as she does in *Rain Clouds*) fails her here when the subject is largely one of love or sexual passion. But on the whole, the dominance of sexual relationships in *Maru* does conform with Head's more direct interest in sexual perception and identity—especially the woman's. As a Masarwa in the middle of a hostile tribe Margaret is the typical Bessie Head exile, living in extreme isolation from her environment, but this feeling of isolation is also intensified by the fact that she is a woman with an unusually independent spirit and by her role as the alienated artist.

Margaret's individualism is the legacy of having been "permanently unwanted by society" and of being forced to develop her own inner resources as a Masarwa and as a woman. That legacy, together with the advantages of having been reared by a remarkably resourceful and independent woman, has given Margaret control "over the only part of her life that would be hers, her mind and soul," and in the process she acquires the capacity for survival "within herself" (p. 16). Her Masarwa features typically resemble a variety of ethnic groups—Chinese, African, and "God knows what" (p. 23)—and this ethnically universal image complements that sense of wholeness and inner strength which is the essence of her individualism and which enables her to reject tribal divisiveness, sexual manipulativeness, and political privileges. It is this sense of inner wholeness that also permits her to maintain her own feeling of individual separateness while sharing her world with friends and even animals (a stray she-goat). These qualities are all evinced by her art as painter, for her work is based on an inner emotional strength which captures the emotional lives, and not merely the physical forms, of her subjects.

In a decidedly more subjective context than that of *Rain Clouds*, Head is dramatizing the central paradox of art and individualism. They are essentially self-conscious, even self-contained, but simultaneously they are committed, in their ideal states, to contact and to harmony with others. Finally, Margaret's individualism and art are intertwined with her perceptions as a woman. Despite her shortcomings (she is narrowly intellectual and afraid of her own emotions) the older Margaret Cadmore represents a self-sufficiency that is striking not only on its own terms but also because she is a woman. Her adopted daughter has succeeded to this rare heritage of an untrammeled individualism in a woman, while combining it with a frank capacity for deep passion and strong imagination. Thus her undeveloped relationship with the dangerous Moleka never really threatens her, because her passion for him is more than offset by the individualistic self-protectiveness which keeps her at a distance from him.

Judged in the light of this female individualism, Dikeledi is less mature than Margaret. In some respects she is unusually unconventional as a woman, deciding, for example, to acquire and actually use her training as a teacher. Her strong personality, together with her contempt for tribal prejudices, makes her a formidable ally for Margaret, but she is also hampered by limited assumptions about sexual identity and roles as these affect the woman, and these assumptions make her easy prey for the unscrupulous Moleka. She loves him as much as Margaret does, but without the other woman's protective self-awareness. Dikeledi is humane enough to be concerned about Moleka's selfish sexuality, but her own sexual posture implies a degree of self-destructiveness, particularly the highly suggestive walk and dress which inevitably lure Moleka to her bed and eventually into a marriage dictated by Maru.

Moleka himself provokes a certain ambivalence in the reader as well as in Margaret. His remarkably forceful personality bespeaks a strength of will that obviously attracts the equally strong-willed Margaret, and his own response to her strength suggests a certain sensitivity in his character. On the other hand, his individualism often takes the form of a narrow egotism and a self-centered masculinity which prey on gullible women. In this regard his personality is a manifestation of that exploitive power which Head invariably locates in the male ego and, by extension, in the entrenched structures of feudal privilege, racism, and tribalism. The undeveloped nature of the mutual attraction which Moleka and Margaret have for each other is consistent with Head's presentation of sexual roles as modes of power. Their mutual attraction confirms their similarities to each other, but the absence of any consummation underscores their differences—Margaret's powerful self-awareness is intrinsic to the ideal womanhood which Head envisions and which contrasts with Moleka's conventional notions of masculinity as possessive power.

If Margaret represents Head's ideal womanhood, then Maru symbolizes an emerging male humaneness. In this sense, the marriage that he engineers with her is allegorically significant. He is the only one who really approximates her humane but powerful individuality, and, like her, he has learned to perceive the analogy between corrupt forms of social power and the kind of exploitive masculinity that marks Moleka. At the same time, he recalls Makhaya of *Rain Clouds* in his revulsion at the kind of manipulative helplessness which many women affect in conventionally "feminine" roles: having chosen women because of their "tender" smile and the "mystery" of their eyes, Maru has often found that "a tender smile and a scheming mind went hand in hand, a beautiful voice turned into a dominating viper who confused the inner Maru" (p. 35). In other words, Maru is as repelled by power in the destructively conventional female as he is alienated by the kind of power-hungry masculinity embodied by Moleka.

On the whole Head invests Maru with a moral ambiguity that is reminiscent of Makhaya's personality in *Rain Clouds*. There is a marked tension between the man's emerging and undeveloped male humaneness and the entrenched masculine need to define itself in terms of power. As a social reformer, Maru is both the idealistic humanist, attacking tribalism, social privileges, and limiting sexual roles, and a manipulative power-broker engineering complex plots for Dikeledi's marriage and his own. He embodies a characteristic tension in Head's fiction between the reformer's idealistic vision and the persistent, limiting realities within and outside the reformer. In spite of the generosity of some of his intentions (protecting Margaret from Moleka, and giving Dikeledi what she has always sought by way of tight skirts), Maru's schemes actually invite comparisons with Moleka the arch manipulator. His benevolent deviousness is really comparable with that manipulative femininity which he despises in conventional women and which he actually exploits in Dikeledi's case by using his sister's calculating suggestiveness as bait for Moleka.

Maru's role as reformist and benevolent schemer raises, in an even more disturbing manner than does Makhaya's role, questions about the social and moral ambiguities of the male as the dominant agent (usually as protector or leader) in the woman's search for her own individualism. In *Rain Clouds*, Paulina's individualism is sufficiently underdeveloped to allow her meek acquiescence in Makhaya's self-proclaimed role as director and protector of her equal status. In *Maru*, Head's scepticism about this kind of compassionate masculinity is more pronounced. There is a marked detachment, on the woman's part, from the man's assumption of the protective role, especially when that woman enjoys the strong self-protectiveness and inner strength of Margaret Cadmore. While Dikeledi's rather limited individuality requires and invites Maru's protective strength, Margaret's independence protects her equally from Maru's protective dominance and Moleka's crude masculinity. Margaret therefore represents a telling detachment from the male's passion for power as domination. In Maru's case, she does not really disguise the fact that her marriage has not ended her love for Moleka. The very persistence of that love, especially on the self-protective basis on which it has always existed, reflects the ideal kind of power which Margaret symbolizes—a firm sense of choices and a certain strength of will. Margaret's uncompromised individuality tends to emphasize that Maru's masculine power is essentially irrelevant to the protective habits of her inner self.

He is not altogether irrelevant, however, because in a more general sense he is an important symbol of the male presence and its impact on the woman's self-awareness. In so far as the question of power and independence is intrinsic to the woman's social role and identity, the very notion of her individuality or equality can only be adequately developed by the woman who frankly deals with the manner in which acts of female self-determination react to, or are influenced by, the pervasiveness and intransigence of male dominance. In Margaret's case she must deal, in an external way, with the subordinating effects of Maru's use of power as a mode of protectiveness and possession, but even more urgently, she must also deal with her attraction to a male power-symbol—Moleka—which is so manifestly destructive and so manifestly contrary to what she believes in for women and men. In this latter sense, Margaret's experience suggests that the woman needs to confront the issue of male power, not only as it has been embodied by the man himself, but more insidiously, as it exists in her own psyche in modes that she has accepted, unwittingly, from the male-oriented conventions of her society. This is the more problematic question of power to which Head's third and most ambitious novel to date addresses itself.

The structure of *A Question of Power* is the most subjective of Head's novels. The entire narrative is filtered through the consciousness of Elizabeth, the main protagonist. Hers is a disturbed consciousness: throughout most of the novel she is suffering from a nervous breakdown and the narrative is actually a description of events as they unfold within her mind and of the relationship between these internal events and the world outside. The outside world is Motabeng, Botswana, where Elizabeth works as a school teacher and then as a member of the local agricultural cooperative. Within Head's narrative design, the social environment and Elizabeth's role within it are presented as periodic interruptions of what is the continuing and dominant reality in the novel—the hallucinations and the painful self-doubts that dramatize Elizabeth's insecurities as a woman who feels threatened by male power and sexuality, and as a South African "colored" who has been told that her white mother died as a patient in a mental hospital. Her hallucinations center upon two male figures, Sello and Dan, who remind her of two men whom she knows vaguely in Motabeng. In her fantasies they are really important as images—her images of male roles and sexual power—which compete with each other for control of her personality. Their struggle, between Sello the symbol of love and compassion and Dan the epitome of destructive male egotism, is developed in the form of a morality play, and this form emphasizes the moral significance of the emotional and intellectual conflicts here.

The very existence of these conflicts is significant in an understanding of Elizabeth's predicament. Her mental breakdown dramatizes the extent to which her society's destructive obsession with power-as-domination has become an integral part of her own psyche. As a victim of that obsession (a lonely "colored" woman in exile from South African apartheid) she has also become its symptom—largely because of the fact that her intense preoccupation with male power reflects the extent to which that power has become a dominant force in her own personality. Consequently, racial conflict has been internalized in her, taking the form of the "colored" person's ethnic insecurities and sense of uprootedness. The male obsession with exploitive power explains her sense of female dependency throughout most of the novel, and her marked uneasiness with sexual passion—she almost invariably envisages sex as a "cesspool"—is an internal reflection of the domineering exploitiveness which corrupts the erotic experience in the world outside.

The imaginary feud between Dan and Sello dramatizes the turmoil in Elizabeth's inner world. It is significant that their living counterparts are really strangers to Elizabeth, because this emphasizes that they are less important as living male individuals than they are as images of the male and of sexual roles within Elizabeth's personality. As images, Dan and Sello emphasize the manner in which Elizabeth perceives men in her world, and the manner in which her perception of men, and theirs of her, have shaped her moral sense, her sexuality, and her individuality as a woman. More specifically, these male images represent the extent to which Elizabeth's self-awareness as a woman has internalized and must now deal with the various nuances of male symbols as the essence of power. They assume a dominant role in her mind, as well as in the narrative as a whole, precisely because the very act of establishing a full-fledged individuality as a woman requires her to confront directly the phenomenon of male power as an internal and corrupting *female* value system.

Dan has a captivating erotic presence which is able to penetrate even the self-defensive coldness with which Elizabeth usually envelops her sexuality. His extreme masculinity attracts her, his touch brings her exquisite sensations, even a heightened ecstasy, and he "made a woman feel like an ancient and knowledgeable queen of love" (pp. 105-06). In responding in this way to Dan's erotic image Elizabeth personifies a continuing female dilemma. An unreserved response to Dan would amount to a self-willed and ultimately self-destructive vulnerability to his exploitive power, but a completely protective reserve would amount to the denial of her sexual needs, thereby encouraging the very kind of longing that makes her susceptible to Dan's sexuality in the first place.

Dan is both a seductive presence and a revolting example of erotic power and ethnic arrogance (as a black man he taunts the racially mixed Elizabeth with his alleged sexual superiority). At the very moment at which she despises his ethnic and sexual taunts as symptoms of her own ethnic and sexual insecurities, she is fascinated by his displays of phallic power—from his habitual gesture of "flaying his powerful penis in the air" (p. 13) to that enormous sexual appetite which leads to all-night love-making and to the exhaustion of his women. Dan does not represent a very serious temptation for Elizabeth; it is easy enough for her to recognize and resist his crude egotism and his sadistic view of women as objects to be used and discarded. The attraction he does hold for her has some significance in her quest for a harmonious rather than conflicting self-awareness. That attraction does imply that she is fascinated with the kind of power represented by the Dan image, and even more crucially, the fact that Dan is an image in her own mind implies that such a power has become intrinsic to the way in which she views herself as a woman. In other words, although his aura of selfish and untrammeled power outrages her moral sense, it also dominates her consciousness and appeals to her precisely because she is so disturbed by her female dependency.

Sello represents a different kind of ambiguity to Elizabeth. At first he appears to her as Dan's unquestionable and clear-cut antithesis: he represents love both as a religious principle (he often appears in the guise of a monk) and as an ideal human capacity to share one's self without destroying the other. As an image of love he represents the universal harmony and individual growth that are the controlling ideals in *Rain Clouds* and *Maru*. Sello's are the ideals to which Elizabeth appeals whenever she rejects Dan's explotive concept of love, or whenever she attacks her favorite political targets—white racism, black nationalism, and condescending white liberals. On the other hand, Sello's role in Elizabeth's imagination and perception brings him closer to Dan than the reader, or Elizabeth, initially assumes. It turns out that the morality-play struggle between Dan and Sello, and even the existence of the Dan image, have been created by Sello himself—in order to test Elizabeth, as Sello informs her after the Dan image has been vanquished. In effect, Sello is another manifestation of the male's ingrained habits of manipulative power—even when that power is directed by benevolent motives, such as saving Margaret Cadmore from Moleka or preserving Elizabeth's psyche from Dan's influence.

The confrontation which Sello engineers with Dan, the image of evil, is essential for Elizabeth's understanding of the nature of moral idealism itself, for moral idealism in its most effective sense must be intimately aware of the realities of evil as well as preoccupied with visions of goodness. On this basis, Dan and Sello are not simply moral antitheses but also opposite sides of a single moral awareness (Elizabeth's). By extension, they reflect the manner in which Head's own narrative viewpoint is motivated by a characteristic tension between moral idealism and social realism. This moral tension within Elizabeth is comparable with the sexual conflicts which Sello's manipulative schemes bring to her attention. She is conventionally dependent, but as her rejection of Dan suggests, she wants to live without anyone dominating her existence.

The fact that it is a male image (Sello) that needs to devise all of this for Elizabeth's enlightenment takes us back to that paradox which is fundamental to the male presence in both *Rain Clouds* and *Maru*: the male's power and leadership are crucial to the process whereby the woman perceives or actually experiences her full individuality and equal role in relation to the man. Once again Head is insisting on the pervasive influence of masculine-oriented notions of power, not only in men and in social institutions, but also within women themselves. If the idea (and rightness) of masculine power has become an active principle within the woman's consciousness, then in Elizabeth's case this means that the very act of attempting to grow into a full individuality depends on her ability to recognize the degree to which her life as a woman is dominated by male power for evil (Dan) as well as for benevolent (Sello) ends. Confronting the facts of male power within her and in the world around her (as usual the cooperative is run by men) is a first step towards achieving her own independent strength, in much the same way that the very process of facing up to her female diffidence about exploring these kinds of things will ensure her eventual ability to overcome that diffidence: "Journeys into the soul are not for women with children, not all that dark heaving turmoil. They are for men" (p. 50).

More specifically, when Elizabeth actually experiences Dan's personality and when she clearly perceives the implications of his image in her society and in her inner life, she is well on the way to thrusting him from his dominant role in her imagination. In Sello's case, her self-critical recognition of the extent to which she has been dependent on him as teacher and manipulative leader initiates her growth into self-reliance. On both counts, she begins to move towards an inner harmony and into harmony with others, a movement which is signalized by the passing of her mental disturbance and by a symbolic gesture at the end of the novel. As she falls asleep for the first time after many nights of hallucinations, "she placed one soft hand over her land. It was a gesture of belonging" (p. 206). In keeping with Head's typical insistence that entrenched evil and inequity do not vanish overnight, this gesture does not mean that Elizabeth or her world has been completely reborn. Elizabeth's growth is new, and is barely beginning when the novel comes to a close. Her maturity into an independent self-awareness proceeds side by side with the dominance of hatred and abusive power in the world around her. In this regard, the juxtaposition of Dan and Sello as images may be applied to society at large. Society is dominated by the intransigent evils represented by the Dan image, while bearing the promise of Sello's moral idealism. Without offering easy guarantees that this promise will be fulfilled, Elizabeth's experience suggests possibilities for a world of new men and women by virtue of raising questions about the old order of things. This is the kind of possibility that has consistently remained the most vital and influential aspect of Head's fiction, shaping not only her moral idealism but her level-headed perception of reality as well.

Conclusion

The importance of private growth as a prerequisite for social change is more explicit in the works of Bessie Head than in the other women writers discussed, but she is representative rather than unique in this regard. In retrospect, all the major writers are pre-occupied with the woman's personal strength—or lack of it—when they analyze sexual roles and sexual inequality. In these works, the victims of inequality and male insensitivity are not only victimized by their external circumstances, they are also at a disadvantage because they lack strength, resourcefulness, and a vital sense of their own integrity as women. Their inner weaknesses often stem from the degree to which they have internalized male modes of perception—until they accept male notions about female inadequacy and about masculine privilege. When they are strong, their strength is portrayed realistically and they do not automatically transcend deep-rooted social barriers simply because they are strong. Their strength allows them to be resilient in dealing with these barriers, however, and it does enable them to remain uncowed by social or individual resistance.

There is a tough-minded realism in all of this. There is no facile sentimentalism here. This emphasis on the woman's individuality cuts two ways. On one hand, strong women like Head's Margaret Cadmore or Nwapa's Efuru represent an admirable refusal to accept the restrictiveness of the status quo, a dogged determination to define their own lives in terms of their own sense of integrity and need. On the other hand, these writers also expose the cramped personalities and narrow perspectives of that female individuality which accepts established restrictions. This explains why Head's Dikeledi *(Maru)* and the women in Aidoo's "Two Sisters" have such limited personalities. They are manipulative women who never really question the custom of female subordination and male privilege—the very custom that encourages women to resort to manipulation and double-dealing in their relationships with men and with each other. In fact, this kind of female manipulativeness actually depends on the status quo of female dependency in order to be effective.

This kind of realism also precludes the kind of facile optimism, about social change, that is so often found in protest literature by victimized groups. Given their hard-headed awareness of the woman's limitations, as well as the limitations of the society around her, these writers offer no easy promises of social revolution or institutional changes. They do not tend to assume, as we so often do in the West, that external social reforms (in the law-books or institutions, for example) will, by themselves, effect meaningful change. Their works clearly imply that profound and pervasive changes can only take place when external reforms go hand in hand with fundamental, personal growth.

This also explains why protest as such is a relatively secondary matter among the major writers. Even a writer like Buchi Emecheta whose protest is the bluntest and most sustained of them all, emphasizes that simply protesting against one's victimization and getting the other to accept responsibility for that victimization are far less important than the business of correcting the effects of inequality and dependency. Most important of all, the burdens of correction and personal growth fall entirely on the shoulders of the victim herself. Paradoxical and difficult—even unfair—as it might seem, she is really the only one who can actually pull herself up from the ditch into which others cast her. And unlikely, and unpromising, as it might seem, as a second class citizen, she must somehow find within her the buried potential to become a first class citizen. In spite of the unevenness of her work, Emecheta is very close to the much more complex Bessie Head in posing this difficult paradox for women who seek to mature into some kind of self-sufficiency. The very nature of female dependency, any dependency for that matter, encourages the habit of leaning on others and on supportive conventions; yet this is the first, most crucial, habit that women like Emecheta's Adah Obi must break, relatively unaided, in the slow and completely unguaranteed growth into independence. There is no cheap or easy pathway here to the brave new world of female equality and integrity. In fact, the road to individual strength is very private, often difficult and lonely.

It is always advisable to qualify statements about individualism and private experience in African literature and culture—although this is not done as often as it should be. Clearly, individual experience and the importance of personal privacy do not always mean the same thing when we move from the highly individualistic West to the traditionally communal cultures of Africa. The significance of these concepts varies from culture to culture, and writer to writer within Africa itself. In the case of the major women writers, Bessie Head is a "colored" South African whose mixed racial background, lack of tribal roots, and personal exile have all ensured a considerable distance, even detachment, from those communal values which we usually associate with tribal cultures in Africa. Buchi Emecheta came out of such a culture—the Ibos of Nigeria—but she is no longer a part of it. For years she has lived and written in England, where she is also a professional sociologist. Both of these writers are much closer to the Westerner's prized mystique of individualism and personal privacy than some of their counterparts.

Flora Nwapa, Efua Sutherland and Ama Ata Aidoo are clearly closer, in emotional terms at the very least, to their tribal cultures. As a result, they approach the issue of female individualism somewhat differently. In their writings, individualism is always tempered by a deep and complex loyalty to the indigenous culture and its own mystique—the mystique of close community ties and sacred family obligations. Consequently, their women, even explicitly rebellious ones like Aidoo's Anowa, must fulfill their individual needs as strong-willed, independent women within, even in spite of, these strong communal traditions. Anowa, Nwapa's rural and urban women, and Sutherland's Ampoma *(Edufa)* they are all engaged in a difficult and demanding balancing act, striving to achieve a fulfilling sense of themselves as distinctive human personalities while remaining loyal to the all-encompassing community around them. It is the kind of balancing act that is invariably beyond the capacities of women in Grace Ogot's more fatalistic or resigned fiction in which it seems impossible to break away from *any* aspect of the traditional community without rupturing the woman's relationship with the entire structure. Here too the question of individual choice, albeit an abortive one, is fairly obvious in Ogot's work.

In spite of the differences between these writers there is always that crucial link—the issue of individual choice. Whether it functions in the de-tribalized, often isolated, context of Head's fictive world, or whether it is firmly located in a vigorous communal tradition, the issue of female individualism remains paramount to all of these writers. They are all concerned with the woman's need for a sense of choice. Whether her search for options takes place in a communal context or a Westernized one, her needs are invariably defined on the basis of some tension with prevailing attitudes towards women.

In concentrating as they do on the woman's sense of her own self, it seems almost inevitable that these writers would be drawn into the related subject of the imagination. The private and social consciousness of their women exemplifies the imagination itself at work. The woman's perception and description of her experience is an imaginative process, the same process through which Efuru or Adah Obi gradually clarifies her needs and individuality. The maturing and the function of individual perception are creative and imaginative processes that are akin to the working of the artistic imagination itself.

Hence in Head's *A Question of Power*, Elizabeth's troubled but creative mind is comparable with the creative power of the artist's imagination. Her total experience in the novel amounts to a gradual creation of a new self. This kind of analogy with artistic creation is also implicit in the drama of Sutherland and Aidoo. Their plays emphasize parallels between their own art—the conventions of the theater itself—and the sexual role-playing through which their women emerge as complex individuals.

Some of the writers go beyond analogy. In *Second Class Citizen*, Buchi Emecheta makes it quite clear that there is no essential difference between Adah Obi's struggle for independence and her attempts to write a novel. Both struggles, to be an individual and a writer, flow from the individual imagination, from imaginative energies that envisage and then proceed to shape the woman's personal needs—and her artistic perception of women like herself. In this respect, we may compare Adah Obi with Margaret Cadmore in Head's *Maru*. The latter's role as artist is indistinguishable from her identity as an unusually perceptive and intensely introverted woman with a strong awareness of her unusual qualities.

The woman's self-conscious attempts to achieve independence merge with the artist's emphasis on the manner in which art and personal growth are intertwined. In fact, this emphasis is beginning to assume a certain self-consciousness of its own. Having established that there is a tradition of female needs and roles, the woman writer in Africa is beginning to establish a parallel tradition—one in which the writer is conscious of belonging to a *tradition* of literature by African women. Thus, Emecheta's Adah Obi can cite the example of a *woman* novelist from Africa—Flora Nwapa—when she defends her own attempts to write a novel (*Second Class Citizen*, p. 167). The African woman writer has now become her own best symbol of female achievement and growth.

Once we establish that there is an entrenched and fairly self-conscious tradition of literature by African women, we still need to clarify the connections, if any, between this specifically African phenomenon and the concurrent phenomena of women's movements and literature, in the West. Clearly, the considerable cultural differences preclude any attempt to forge easy, all-embracing comparisons between the specific criteria of Western feminists and the judgements by women writers in black Africa. It would be unrealistic to expect a uniform political objective among African women when such a uniformity is so palpably absent among Western feminists.

Bessie Head and Buchi Emecheta, for example, are equally militant in attacking female subordination in Africa, but Emecheta is far more naive than is Head about the political and social status of the Western, middle-class woman. On the whole, however, it is possible to detect a common preoccupation with the woman's need for a fulfilled and unrestricted personality. This common preoccupation among the African writers not only transcends the specific differences between them, it also facilitates comparisons with Western feminism, in the broadest sense of the term—feminism as a search for the woman's social equality and individual fulfillment in the West.

Altogether, the African writer reflects an uneasiness or outright hostility towards the sociosexual status quo, and this attitude is broadly comparable with the various forms of political activism and literary protest by Western feminists. The point is not that African women necessarily share identical political objectives with each other or with Western feminists. What makes them of special interest to both non-African and African readers at this time is the fact that, despite differences, they are engaged in a searching and critical enquiry into the quality of women's lives, while raising pointed questions about the shortcomings of entrenched social attitudes. Such an enquiry deserves careful study on its own merit, but at a time when the needs and experiences of women have become global concerns, the questions raised by these African women seem especially compelling and appropriate.

Notes

Notes to Chapter 1

1. Marie Linton-Umeh, "The African Heroine," in *Sturdy Black Bridges: Visions of Black Women in Literature*, eds. Roseann P. Bell, Bettye J. Parker, and Beverly Guy-Sheftall (New York: Doubleday, 1979), pp. 39-51.

2. Efua Sutherland, in a letter to the author (June 2, 1976).

3. Léopold Sédar Senghor, *Prose and Poetry*, selected and trans. by John Reed and Clive Wake (London: Oxford University Press, 1965), pp. 44-45.

4. See, for example, Douglas Killam, "Cyprian Ekwensi," in *Introduction to Nigerian Literature*, ed. Bruce King (Lagos: University of Lagos, 1971), pp. 87-90; Adrian Roscoe, *Mother Is Gold: A Study in West African Literature* (Cambridge, England: Cambridge University Press, 1971), pp. 90-93.

5. Sylvia Washington Bâ, *The Concept of Negritude in the Poetry of Léopold Sédar Senghor* (Princeton: Princeton University Press, 1973), p. 53.

6. Chinua Achebe, *Things Fall Apart*, African Writers Series Ed. (London: Heinemann, 1962), pp. 121-22.

7. Ousmane Sembène, *God's Bits of Wood*, trans. Francis Price, Anchor Books Ed. (New York: Doubleday, 1970), pp. 75-76.

8. O. R. Dathorne, *The Black Mind: A History of African Literature* (Minneapolis: University of Minnesota Press, 1974), pp. 206-07. Dathorne also discusses Grace Ogot (pp. 220-21), Gladys Casely-Hayford (pp. 251-52), Sutherland (pp. 259-60, 415, 419), and Aidoo (pp. 425, 428).

9. Elizabeth Gunner, "Songs of Innocence and Experience: Women as Composers and Performers of *IZIBONGO*, Zulu Praise Poetry," *Research in African Literatures*, 10, 2 (1979), 239-67.

10. Maryse Conde, "Three Female Writers in Modern Africa: Flora Nwapa, Ama Ata Aidoo and Grace Ogot," *Presence Africaine* 2, no. 82 (1972), 132-43.

11. Femi Ojo-Ade, "Bessie Head's Alienated Heroine: Victim or Villain?" *Ba Shiru*, 8, 2 (1977), 13-21.

12. Donald Bayer Burness, "Womanhood in the Short Stories of Ama Ata Aidoo," *Studies in Black Literature*, 4, 2 (1973), 21-24.

Notes to Chapter 2

1. *Poems from Black Africa*, ed. Langston Hughes, Midland Book Edition (Bloomington, Indiana: Indiana University Press, 1966), p. 31.

2. Pallo Jordan, "Foreword," in *Tales from Southern Africa*, trans. A. C. Jordan, introd. Harold Scheub (Berkeley, California: University of California Press, 1973), pp. xv-xvii.

3. Aquah Laluah, "Nativity," in *Poems from Black Africa* (pp. 76-77).

4. Barbara Kimenye, *Kalasanda Revisited* (London: Oxford University Press, 1966), pp. 39-52.

5. Barbara Kimenye, *Kalasanda* (London: Oxford University Press, 1965), pp. 97-99.

6. Adaora Lily Ulasi, *Many Thing You No Understand*, Fontana Books Ed. (London: Collins, 1973), p. 35.

7. Adaora Lily Ulasi, *Many Thing Begin for Change*, Fontana Books Ed. (London: Collins, 1975), p. 153.

8. Adelaide Casely-Hayford, "Mista Courifer," in *An African Treasury*, ed. Langston Hughes, Pyramid Books Ed. (New York: Pyramid Books, 1961), p. 138.

9. Mabel Dove-Danquah, "Anticipation," in *An African Treasury* (pp. 159-62).

10. Noemia de Sousa, "Appeal," in *Modern Poetry from Africa*, eds. Gerald Moore and Ulli Beier. Penguin Ed. (Harmondsworth, England: Penguin, 1963), p. 239.

11. Marina Gashe, "The Village," in *Poems from Black Africa* (p. 47).

12. Medard Kasese, "Black Mother," *New Writing from Zambia*, No. 7, 2 (1971), 22.

13. Micere Githae-Mugo, "Wife of the Husband," *Okike: An African Journal of New Writing*, no. 4 (December, 1973), 78.

14. Francesca Yetunde Pereira, "Two Strange Worlds," in *Poems from Black Africa* (p. 94).

15. References to Ogot's work are based on *The Promised Land* (Nairobi, Kenya: East African Publishing, 1966), and *Land Without Thunder* (Nairobi, Kenya: East African Publishing House, 1968).

16. Patience Henaku Addo, *Company Pot*, in *Nine African Plays for Radio*, eds. Gwyneth Henderson and Cosmo Pieterse (London: Heinemann, 1973), pp. 163-85.

Notes to Chapter 3

1. References to Emecheta's works are based on *In the Ditch* (London: Barrie and Jenkins, 1972); *Second Class Citizen*, Amer. Ed. (New York: George Braziller, 1975); *The Bride Price* (London: Allison and Busby, 1976); and *The Slave Girl* (London: Allison and Busby, 1977).
2. See, for example, Alice Walker, "A Writer of, not in spite of, her Children," *Ms* (January, 1976), 40, 106.
3. Compare Betty Friedan, *The Feminine Mystique* (New York: W. W. Norton, 1963).

Notes to Chapter 4

1. *African Writers Talking: A Collection of Radio Interviews*, ed. Cosmo Pieterse and Dennis Duerden (New York: Africana Publishing Corporation, 1972), pp. 188-89, 22. Cited hereafter in the text as *African Writers Talking*.
2. References to Sutherland's plays are based on *Edufa* in *Plays from Black Africa*, ed. Frederic M. Litto, Mermaid Edition (New York: Hill & Wang, 1968), pp. 209-72; *Foriwa* (Accra: Ghana State Publishing Corporation, 1967) and *The Marriage of Anansewa*, African Creative Writing Series (London: Longman, 1975).
3. Francis Fergusson, *The Idea of a Theater*. Anchor Books Ed. (New York: Doubleday, 1953), pp. 14-15.
4. Efua Sutherland, "New Life at Kyerefaso," in *Modern African Prose*, ed. Richard Rive, African Writers Series (London: Heinemann, 1964), pp. 179-86.

Notes to Chapter 5

1. References to Aidoo's plays are based on *The Dilemma of a Ghost* (Accra: Longman, 1965) and *Anowa* (London: Longman, 1970).
2. William R. Bascom, *African Dilemma Tales* (The Hague: Mouton, 1975), p. 1.
3. Donald Bayer Burness, "Womanhood in the Short Stories of Ama Ata Aidoo," *Studies in Black Literature*, 4, 2 (Summer, 1973), 21-24. On the other hand, Ezekiel Mphahlele praises Aidoo for her ability to switch

"naturally" from one point of view to another. See "Introduction," in *No Sweetness Here*, Anchor Books ed. (New York: Doubleday, 1972), p. xiv.

4. "Last of the Proud Ones," *Okyeame*, 2, 1 (1964), 9-10.

5. References to Aidoo's short stories are based on the collection, *No Sweetness Here* (London: Longman, 1970).

Notes to Chapter 6

1. "This is Lagos," in *This Is Lagos and other Stories* (Enugu, Nigeria: Nwankwo-Ifejika, 1971,), p. 10. Further references to Nwapa's short stories are based on this text.

2. Jomo Kenyatta, *Facing Mount Kenya: The Tribal Life of the Gikuyu*, introd. B. Malinowski, Vintage Books Ed. (New York: Random House, n.d.), pp. 117-18.

3. James Olney, *Tell Me Africa: An Approach to African Literature* (Princeton: Princeton University Press, 1973), p. 11.

4. References to Nwapa's novels are based on *Efuru*, African Writers Series (London: Heinemann, 1966); *Idu*, African Writers Series (London: Heinemann, 1970).

Notes to Chapter 7

1. Bessie Head, "Witchcraft," *Ms*, 4, 5 (November, 1975), 73-74.

2. References to Head's novels are based on *When Rain Clouds Gather*, Bantam Edition (New York: Bantam Books, 1970); *Maru*, African Writers Series (London: Heinemann, 1972); and *A Question of Power*, African Writers Series (London: Heinemann, 1974).

3. *Ms*, 4, 5 (November, 1975), 73-74.

Bibliography

This bibliography deals only with those titles and sources which include women writers in black Africa. It is not intended to be a source guide to African literature in general. Titles published too late for discussion in this study are not included here.

Primary Sources

Ghana

Addo, Joyce. "On Parting" and "Patriotism." In *Voices of Ghana: Literary Contributions to the Ghana Broadcasting System*. Accra, Ghana: Ghana Broadcasting System, 1958, pp. 202, 216.

Addo, Patience Henaku. *Company Pot*, In *Nine African Plays for Radio*. African Writers Series. London: Heinemann, 1973, pp. 163-85.

Aidoo, Ama Ata. *Anowa*. London: Longman, 1970.

―――. "Cornfields in Accra." In *The Word Is Here*. Ed. Keorapatse Kgositsile New York: Doubleday, 1973, pp. 113-16.

―――― *Dilemma of a Ghost*. Accra, Ghana: Longman, 1965.

―――. "Last of the Proud Ones." *Okyeame* 2, no. 1 (1964), pp. 9-10.

―――. "No Sweetness Here." London: Longman, 1970.

Dove-Danquah, Mabel. "Anticipation." In *An African Treasury: Essays Stories Poems By Black Africans*. Ed. Langston Hughes. New York: Pyramid, 1961, pp. 159-62.

Laluah, Aquah. "Shadow of Darkness" and "Nativity." In *Poems from Black Africa*. Ed. Langston Hughes. Midland Book Ed. Bloomington, Ind.: Indiana University Press, 1966, pp. 75, 76.

―――― "The Serving Girl." In *An African Treasury: Essays Stories Poems*

By Black Africans. Ed. Langston Hughes. New York: Pyramid, 1961, p. 177.

Ngatho, Stella. "Footpath," "The Kraal" and "A Young Tree." In *The Word Is Here.* Ed. Keorapatse Kgositsile. New York: Doubleday, 1973, pp. 32-33.

Sutherland, Efua. *Edufa.* In *Plays from Black Africa.* Ed. Frederic M. Litto. Mermaid Ed. New York: Hill & Wang, 1968, pp. 209-72.

_____ *Foriwa.* Accra, Ghana: State Publishing Corporation, 1967.

_____ "New Life at Kyerefaso." In *An African Treasury*, pp. 112-17.

_____ *The Marriage of Anansewa.* London: Longman, 1975.

Kenya

Githae-Mugo, Micere. "Wife of the Husband." *Okike*, no. 4 (December, 1973), p. 78.

Jillings, Harriet. "Ngethe." *Busara*, 3, 2 (1971), pp. 10-12.

Khamadi, Miriam. "They Ran Out of Mud" and "On Wings." *Transition*, no. 25, 2 (1966), p. 22.

Ndegwa, Catherine. "The Revelation." *Busara*, 2, 3 (1969), pp. 23-26.

Njaw, Elimo (Marina Gashe). "The Village." In *Poems from Black Africa* ed. Langston Hughes. Midland Book Ed. Bloomington, Ind.: Indiana University Press, 1966, p. 47.

Ogada, Penniah. "A Case for Inheritance." In *More Modern African Stories.* Ed. Charles R. Larson. Fontana Books Ed. London: Collins, 1975, pp. 113-20.

Ogot, Grace. *The Promised Land.* Nairobi, Kenya: East African Publishing House, 1966.

_____ *Land Without Thunder.* Nairobi, Kenya: East African Publishing House, 1968.

Mozambique

De Sousa, Noemia. "Appeal," in *Modern Poetry from Africa.* eds. Gerald Moore and Ulli Beier. Harmondsworth, England: Penguin, 1963, pp. 239-40.

Nigeria

Emecheta, Buchi. *In The Ditch.* London: Barrie & Jenkins, 1972.

_____ *Second Class Citizen.* American Ed. New York: George Braziller, 1975.

_____ *The Bride Price.* London: Allison & Busby, 1976.

_____ *The Slave Girl.* London: Allison & Busby, 1977.

Nwapa, Flora. *Efuru*. African Writers Series. London: Heinemann, 1966.
_____ *Idu*. African Writers Series. London: Heinemann, 1970.
_____ *This Is Lagos and Other Stories*. Enugu, Nigeria: Nwankwo-Ifejika, 1971.
Pereira, Francesca Yetunde. "The Paradox," "Mother Dark," "The Burden," "Two Strange Worlds." In *Poems from Black Africa* ed. Langston Hughes. Midland Bank Ed. Bloomington, Ind.: Indiana University Press, 1966, pp. 90-95.
Segun, Mabel. "The Pigeon Hole," "Conflict," "Corruption," "A Second Olympus." In *Reflections: Nigerian Prose and Verse*. Lagos: African Universities Press, 1962, pp. 64-67.
Ulasi, Adaora Lily. *Many Thing Begin For Change*. Fontana ed. London: Collins, 1975.
_____ *Many Thing You No Understand*. Fontana ed. London: Collins, 1973.

Sierra Leone

Casely-Hayford, Adelaide. "Mista Courifer." In *Modern African Stories*. eds. Ayitey Komey and Ezekiel Mphahlele. London: Faber & Faber, 1964, pp. 50-59.

South Africa

Head, Bessie. *A Question of Power*. African Writers Series. London: Heinemann, 1974.
_____ *Maru*. African Writers Series. London: Heinemann, 1972.
_____ "The Green Tree." In Contemporary African Literature. eds. Edris Makward and Leslie Lacy. New York: Random House, 1972, pp. 117-20.
_____ "The Prisoner Who Wore Glasses." In *More Modern African Stories*. Ed. Charles R. Larson. Fontana Books Ed. London: Collins, 1975, pp. 42-48.
_____ *When Rain Clouds Gather*. Bantam Ed. New York: Bantam Books, 1970.
_____ "Witchcraft," *Ms* (November, 1975), 73-74.

Uganda

Datta, Saroj. "The Dead Bird." In *Poems from East Africa*. Eds. David Cook and David Rubadiri. African Writers Series. London: Heinemann, 1971, p. 35.

El-Miskery, Sheikha. "The Crack" and "Just a Word." In *Poems from East Africa* Eds. David Cook and David Rubadiri. African Writers Series. London: Heinemann, 1971, pp. 36-37.

Kimenye, Barbara. *Kalasanda*. London: Oxford University Press, 1965.

_____ *Kalasanda Revisited*. London: Oxford University Press, 1966.

Kokunda, Violet. "Kefa Kazania." In *Origin East Africa* ed. David Cook. African Writers Series. London: Heinemann, 1965, pp. 1-3.

Rwakyaka, Proscovia. "The Beard" and "The Inmates." In *Poems from East Africa* Eds. David Cook and David Rubidiri. African Writers Series London: Heinemann, 1971, pp. 147-48.

Zambia

Cannam, Peggie. "The Dog Outside." *New Writing from Zambia*, 7, 4 (December, 1971), p. 27.

Kasese, Medard. "A Prisoner of Inactivity" and "Black Mother." *New Writing from Zambia*, 7, 2 (June, 1971), pp. 22-24.

_____ "A Spectacle" and "An Angler's Treaty." *New Writing from Zambia*, No. 2 (1969), pp. 18-19.

_____ "Mother Bird" and "The Desolate Woman." *New Writing from Zambia*, 7, 1 (March, 1971), pp. 30-31.

_____ "Virgin's Alarm," "Chief Bukunkwel's Political Dirge," "Secret Cult." *New Writing from Zambia*, 6, 2 (November, 1970), pp. 26-29.

Phiri, Irene. "A Wish After Death." *New Writing from Zambia*, 7, 4 (December, 1971), p. 27.

Secondary Sources

Brown, Lloyd W. "Ama Ata Aidoo: The Art of the Short Story and Sexual Roles in Africa." *World Literature Written in English*, 13, no. 2 (November, 1974), pp. 172-84. Discusses relationship between narrative techniques and womanhood themes in Aidoo's short fiction.

_____ "The African Woman as Writer." *Canadian Journal of African Studies*, 9, no. 3 (1975), pp. 493-501. An overview of protest and identity themes in literature by African women.

Bruner, Charlotte. "Been-to or Has-Been: A Dilemma for Today's African Woman." *Ba-Shiru*, 8, no. 2 (1977), pp. 23-31. Discusses the perception of sexual role-changes in the short stories of Aidoo, Head, Nwapa, and Ogot.

Burness, Donald Bayer. "Womanhood in the Short Stories of Ama Ata

Aidoo." *Studies in Black Literature*, 4, no. 2 (Summer, 1973), pp. 21-24. A brief survey of Aidoo's characteristic themes. Claims that she is unique in her concentration on African women, and that she has not mastered her short-story form.

Chapman, Karen C. "Introduction" to Ama Ata Aidoo's *Dilemma of a Ghost*. In *Sturdy Black Bridges: Visions of Black Women in Literature*. eds. Roseann P. Bell, Bettye J. Parker and Beverly Guy-Sheftall. New York: Doubleday, 1979, pp. 25-38. Examines Aidoo's play as a contribution to Ghanaian theater.

Conde, Maryse. "Three Female Writers in Modern Africa: Flora Nwapa, Ama Ata Aidoo and Grace Ogot." *Presence Africaine*, no. 82 (1972), pp. 132-43. Argues that Nwapa and Aidoo are more critical and less conventional than Ogot in their approach to sexual roles and identity.

Dathorne, O. R. *The Black Mind: A History of African Literature*. Minneapolis: University of Minnesota Press, 1974. Includes brief notes on Aidoo, Nwapa, Ogot and Sutherland.

Gunner, Elizabeth. "Songs of Innocence and Experience: Women as Composers and Performers of IZIBONGO, Zulu Praise Poetry." *Research in African Literatures*, 10, no. 2 (Fall, 1979), pp. 239-67. Describes the contribution of women to oral poetry in Zulu culture.

Jordan, A. C. *Tales from Southern Africa*. Berkeley, California: University of California Press, 1973. Includes foreword by Z. Pallo Jordan who explains the dominant role of women in the traditional oral literatures of southern Africa.

Larson, Charles. *The Novel in the Third World*. Washington, D.C.: Inscape, 1976. Includes remarks on Bessie Head, in the context of anticolonial, Third World literature.

Linton-Umeh, Marie. "The African Heroine." In *Sturdy Black Bridges: Visions of Black Women in Literature*, pp. 39-51. Discusses the African woman's image in literature by African men.

Mphahlele, Ezekiel. "Introduction" to Ama Ata Aidoo. *No Sweetness Here*. Anchor Books Ed. New York: Doubleday, 1972, pp. ix-xxiv. Concludes that Aidoo's stories celebrate womanhood in general and motherhood in particular.

Nagenda, John. "Ama Ata Aidoo, J. C. de Graft and R. Sarif Easmon." In *Protest and Conflict in African Literature*, eds. Cosmo Pieterse and Donald Munro. London: Heinemann, 1969, pp. 101-08. Includes analysis of the conflicts between generations and cultures in Aidoo's *Dilemma of a Ghost*.

Ogunba, Oyin. "Modern Drama in West Africa." In *Perspectives on African Literature*. London: Heinemann, 1971, pp. 81-105. Compares and contrasts Efua Sutherland's *Edufa* with Euripides' *Alcestis*.

Ojo-Ade, Femi. "Bessie Head's Alienated Heroine: Victim or Villain?" *Ba-Shiru* 8, no. 2 (1971), pp. 13-21. Dismisses sexual protest as such, as an important issue in Bessie Head's fiction.

Pieterse, Cosmo and Dennis Duerden, eds. *African Writers Talking: A Collection of Radio Interviews*. New York: Africana, 1972. Includes interviews with Aidoo and Sutherland.

Roscoe, Adrian A. *Mother Is Gold: A Study in West African Literature*. Cambridge, England: Cambridge University Press, 1971. Includes brief references to Aidoo and Nwapa.

Stewart, Danièle. "Ghanaian Writing in Prose: A Critical Survey," *Presence Africaine*, No. 91, 3 (1974), pp. 73-105. Refers to social realism in Aidoo's short stories.

Index

Achebe, Chinua, 8-9, 21, 136
Addo, Patience Henaku, 31-32
African literary criticism, male
orientation of, 4-5
African literature: studies of, 3,
10-13; woman's image in, 5
African women: freedom of, 6-7;
idealization of, by male writers,
7-9; status of, 8; white, as
writers, 9-10; as writers, 3-6, 10-
13, 184-185
Aidoo, Ama Ata, 4, 7, 84-121, 159,
182-183; *Anowa*, 56, 90-99; bio-
graphical details, 84-85; "Certain
Winds From the South," 108-
110; critical studies of, 10-11, 12;
The Dilemma of a Ghost, 85-90;
"Everything Counts," 118-119;
"For Whom Things Did Not
Change," 114-116, 117; "A Gift
from Somewhere," 104-108, 116,
117; "In the Cutting of a Drink,"
101-104; individualism of, 182;
"Last of the Proud Ones," 100-
101; "The Message," 112-114,
116-117; "No Sweetness Here,"

116-118; and oral tradition, 99-
100; protest writings of, 22, 33;
realism of, 120; short stories of,
13, 100-121; slavery theme, 56,
91-92; "Something to Talk
About on the Way to the
Funeral," 108, 110-112; theater,
idea of, 61-64; "Two Sisters,"
119-121, 181
Alcestis (Euripides), 65-68
Alienation, social, in Head's
writings, 159-160
Amadi, Elechi, 21-22
Ananse and the Dwarf Brigade
(Sutherland, Efua), 65
Ananse stories, 79
Anansegoro, 79-80
Anowa (Aidoo, Ama Ata), 56,
90-99
"Anticipation" (Dove-Danquah,
Mabel), 23-24
Apartheid, 158
"Appeal" (de Sousa, Noemia), 24
Artistic imagination, 183-184;
Head's views of, 168-169, 170
Ashanti storytelling traditions, 79

ABOUT THE AUTHOR

LLOYD W. BROWN Is Professor of Comparative Literature at the University of Southern California in Los Angeles. His previous books include *Bits of Ivory: Narrative Techniques in Jane Austen's Fiction*, *The Black Writer in Africa and the Americas*, *West Indian Poetry*, and *Amiri Baraka*.